C000212435

CaymanHavana

Elizabeth Brown

The amazing sequence of events recounted
in
This Story is True

Fleet Publishing

for Joanna

with best wishes.

CaymanHavana

The True Story of a Horse's Return

x

[illegible] Brown

26 July 2017

First published in The United Kingdom in 2012 by Fleet Publishing Ltd

www.fleetpublishing.com
email: info@fleetpublishing.com
Fleet Publishing Ltd. PO Box 6748, Wolverhampton WV6 6FF
Registered in England and Wales with company number 7482057

"CaymanHavana" is a true story about real people and animals. Save where information is already in the public domain, each living person and organisation specifically identified in this book, has approved publication of their name and references to them. Names have been changed only where it has been impractical to trace individuals to obtain their permission to use their actual names.

ISBN: 978-0-9570014-3-5

A CIP catalogue record for this title is available from the British Library.

Typeset by Troubador Publishing, Leicester
Printed and bound by CPI, Croydon

Photographic editing (except "Our best showjumping photograph") and cover design by Depinder Juttla

Photographs reproduced with kind permission of copyright owners:
"Our best showjumping photograph" © Eqipics
"This was Falconwood!" © Jane Roberts

All other photographs courtesy of the author.
Painting "Hey Cayman" © Kia Balle Kristensen

ACKNOWLEDGEMENTS

I am confident that all of these people do know how hugely grateful, in many different ways, I am to them. However, I should like to re-emphasise my gratitude to:

Pat and Ted Brown, Edward Evans, the late Prof. Barry Edwards, Dr. Dylan Gorvy, Judith Heywood, all at Gunstone Hall, Alison Goodwin, Gillian Mackay, Sarah Dakin, Kia and Kris Balle Kristensen, Lisa Smith, Jennifer Blenkiron, Susan Maguire, Alison Whitehurst, Sharon Moules Houghton (née Moules Jones), Alex McEachern, Robin ap Cynan, Terry Jones, Dr. Richard Majors, Laraine Beranic, Jules Rendall, Ricky (the improving horseman)

… and almost every day, I thank CaymanHavana for the choice he made.

CONTENTS

ILLUSTRATIONS

Dedicated to

Mrs B.

My mother
and most courageous riding partner.

CaymanHavana

The True Story of a Horse's Return

Chapter One

LAST TURN OUT

On 9th August 2006, I turned Cayman out. As we walked from the yard, I held his lead rope with my left hand – my right hand was on his withers. I teased him about turning into a camel as his withers seemed to be growing more prominent. At 17hh, he was ***nearly*** as tall as a camel. He listened.

I was in a rush as I was going on holiday to Cuba that afternoon; Cayman was in a rush to eat grass. I had left the cheque for the farrier and my mother Mrs B. would take charge.

On 11th August, Cayman developed colic. He had been grazing in the field, walked up the lane normally and then, as soon as he was in his stable, tried to roll. His symptoms were instantly recognized, the vet was called and he was moved to the indoor school. Within two hours of the vet arriving, Cayman was at Liverpool University's Equine Hospital, eighty miles away, undergoing surgery performed by one of the world's leading equine colic surgeons. Cayman's displaced and twisted gut could not be saved. His was one of the worst cases of one of the worst types of colic. Mr and Mrs B. agreed to his euthanasia.

Unlike when Cayman went away on loan to Rodbaston Agricultural College, Corris, Cayman's companion, has not demanded to know where he is; Corris is perfectly settled.

Cayman's four-and-a-half-year-old 'groom', Leah, was told by her parents that Cayman had gone to live with the moon and the stars. The next time that it thundered, Leah said that she could hear Cayman clomping about in the sky.

Harrison, Cayman's Shire cross Thoroughbred friend who, at 17.2hh, is even taller than him, had a commemorative canter – he is still not too keen on galloping – on Cayman's favourite bridle path, The Long Mile, in his memory.

Each time I turned Cayman out, I said goodbye, told him to be good and told him when I would be back. 9th August was the only occasion when I did not do so. I am glad that I did not. *I feel that we have not left each other – and that we never will.*

* * * * * * *

I wrote my first book "CaymanStar", the story of Cayman's life, backwards. This account of our last turn out was written first, while the pain of Cayman's death was raw. I intended it to be the closing chapter of "CaymanStar". I left it out because it made me so sad. It is right that "Last Turn Out" should be the beginning of "CaymanHavana". You will see why ...

"Cayman … my rock"

Chapter Two

DARKNESS

Suicide seemed logical. It wasn't the *first* thing I thought of when Mrs B. told me. She came through the porch and was about two inches into the sitting room when she said:

"It's Cayman; he's gone – colic."

My first thought surprised me. I felt ashamed as I realised that it was relief!

"Now I won't have to worry about him any more."

Mrs B.'s voice was gentle, as she hugged me:

"No, you won't ever have to worry about him, he's safe where he's gone."

I had worried about leaving Cayman. Before we had gone on holiday to Cuba, I had made arrangements for him to go back 'to school' at Rodbaston Agricultural College, on loan, at the end of August. Gemma, the yard manager, had not hesitated to agree and the students were looking forward to having him back. I had decided that I really should go to Dubai to be with my husband, but I did not want to leave Cayman and felt very unsettled. I'm sure that other horse-owners will recognize this 'horse? – partner? – horse?' dilemma.

Then, the meaning of "gone" hit me. I sobbed and sobbed. Mrs B. continued to hold me. I had never cried like that before in my life. After a while, a new and very powerful feeling came over me. I felt that I was fighting a restraint which was manacling both my body and my spirit. I wanted to go with him! I wanted to be *with Cayman*. The pull towards him was immense, inevitable and irresistible. From just below my breastbone I felt a sensation I had never experienced before, as if a strong, thick, umbilical cord looped out into the endless starry darkness of space connecting me to him. The fact that I had a loving family, husband and friends was irrelevant. I wanted to *go with Cayman.*

The next morning I was sure that if I went and looked in the field Cayman would be there, or at least he would be when I had had a good look. It's a big field, surely he'd be there in it, somewhere. He'd be grazing peacefully, the grinding of his huge jaw rhythmical as he systematically mowed the pasture. He would sense that I was there and look up, slightly surprised. His eyes would be soft and his expression enquiring, as he walked slowly but deliberately towards me – still chewing. He *would* be there, I just needed to go and look.

Two parts of my mind were tussling with each other. It was an unequal fight, when my body joined in. My body was in pain, it yearned to search the field, to find him, to put my arms up each side of his strong shoulders and press my face into his neck, to feel his silky coat and smell his warmth again.

By three in the afternoon, I was still in my dressing gown; this seemed quite normal – what was the point of getting dressed? What was the point of anything? Judy arrived. Judy has known me since I was nine. Her face was grave. She had heard that a horse at Gunstone had died; she had feared that it may be Cayman. My mother's note through her letterbox confirmed her fears. Knowing that Cayman was my rock, Judy had anticipated my devastation. She came armed with a big bouquet. The complete understanding of such a good friend was a relief.

As Judy was leaving, she lamented:

"Enzo will miss your Cayman stories." Enzo is Judy's friend, he is from industrial Turin and not at all accustomed to pets, large or small. He was fascinated by my relationship with my horse. Firstly, that it existed at all and, secondly, by its depth and by the diversity of its manifestations. Enzo knew that the simple question (in his charming accent):

"Haweesa Cay-man?" would instantly illuminate my face and push up my cheeks in a smile. He also knew that in response to this question, I could easily still be talking forty minutes later. My husband Ricky had long since learned to ask the same question in a different way. His version was:

"How is Cayman? *In three minutes*!" If I exceeded the time limit, he would cut in:

"Good – I just wanted to know that he is alive and eating well." Poor Ricky, he is not at all horsey; it took him years to learn how to put Cayman's head collar on the right way up. Cayman would stand patiently as Ricky attempted to do up the headpiece under Cayman's jaw, as if it was a throat lash. Cayman liked any sort of fuss and, for him, even having his head collar put on upside down constituted fuss. Cayman liked Ricky, and Ricky knew that if Cayman was happy, I was happy.

The phrase 'Cayman stories' ignited something. I felt as if a light bulb above my head had been switched on. Now I knew what to do with the nine years of memories and all of the emotions which, with the momentum and vibrant colours of an uncontrollable fairground ride, were hurtling around my mind; I would write Cayman stories! That way I would never lose my horse.

I did not leave the house for a week, except late one night to go to the cinema. It was dark in the cinema, that was good, but I did not enjoy the film. Although it was late summer, in my heart it was dark, cruel midwinter. At about 6 p.m. each evening, I would glance over my shoulder at the kitchen clock; it was fetching-in time, but I had no horse to fetch in. I sat at the kitchen table for hours, I felt close to Cayman as I wrote; it was all I wanted to do.

I received some very touching 'in sympathy' cards, they really did help. It dawned on me that I had suffered a bereavement. Now I understood what it meant. How fortunate I had been never to have suffered such an experience before. My friend

Gill is a riding instructor and a psychologist. I was grateful for her gentle, sympathetic telephone call.

Edward was only seventeen when I gave him the saddle and Cayman's best blue numnah, so that he could ride him whilst I was away. Cayman liked Edward, he is calm and gentle. My teacher, Helen, taught Edward to ride. He rides in an elegant, classical way, which made Cayman look lovely.

Poor Edward, he had gone with his friend Laura-Jayne to ride Cayman on 11th August and ended up leading him round and round the indoor school until the vet came. Edward and Laura-Jayne tried to keep Cayman on his feet, or to get him back onto his feet as he repeatedly flung himself on the ground, groaning and writhing, desperately trying to rid himself of the agony of his twisted gut.

As Edward stood outside the porch with the saddle and numnah, the morning after we got back from Cuba, he must have been so anxious. What bravery it took to hand the unused saddle back to me. Ricky let Edward in and Edward put the saddle down on the floor. We hugged each other. I don't know which of us felt more sorry for the other. I felt so sorry that Edward had gone through such an awful ordeal. Edward felt sorry for the sledgehammer of shock that I had suffered upon returning home. We both missed Cayman.

Sarah (Harrison's person), came to see me. Her vast empathy was nearly tangible.

"I expected all the curtains to be closed! If that happened to Harry I don't know what I'd do; I'd stay in bed, I wouldn't want to see anyone." I was fortunate that so many people knew and loved Cayman; their support helped.

Mrs B. had told me that the vets who had treated Cayman said that if I wanted to go up to Liverpool Veterinary Hospital to talk to them, I could. It was important to me to go to Liverpool. It had all happened without me. Mrs B.'s account, her clear explanation and her professional understanding of anatomy, together with my own reading, meant that my questions were already answered. The reason that I had to go to Liverpool was to see what Cayman saw, to be in the last place that he was in, to share something of his last experiences, to be closer to him.

Arrangements were made to go to Liverpool on Friday 1st September, exactly three weeks after Cayman went there. Ricky would take me; I needed to share the experience with him too. On the morning of 1st September, it occurred to me that Edward should be given the opportunity to come as well. He had suffered such a shock. It may help him to see what happened next after the poor horse – whom he had tried to lead round the indoor school, and had willed desperately not to keep dropping onto his side in such acute distress – had eventually been filled with painkiller and sedative by the vet and wrenched away from his home at Gunstone, for ever. Edward was glad of the chance to come with us to Liverpool.

The journey was long; I was all the more amazed at how quickly Sam had managed to do it in the lorry.

We had arranged to see Dr Dylan Gorvy, who had operated on Cayman with Professor Barry Edwards. Getting a bit lost and missing a turning had made us late and Dr Gorvy was due to be on duty so time was short, but he was sympathetic and helpful. It was interesting and informative to be shown computer simulations of different types of equine colic. Dr Gorvy told me that Professor Edwards, one of the world's leading equine colic surgeons, had said that Cayman's had been one of the worst cases, of one of the worst types of colic, he had seen. Poor Cayman – although I could not help feeling un-surprised – Cayman did not do anything by halves! The computer models were fascinating. Dr Gorvy was sensitive in his explanations, I could see that whenever he thought that I was concentrating on the screen he cast a quick sideways glance at me, I think that it was to see whether I looked too upset. I appreciated his sensitivity, but I was alright, the information which I was gaining was interesting, it helped me to feel more involved.

I think that Dr Gorvy was surprised when, having seen the computer models, I announced:

"Now may I see the operating theatre." It was not a question. It was an imperative.

I had to see what Cayman saw. I did not want to be excluded from anything.

We were shown the weighbridge where, for the

purpose of calculating the level of anaesthesia, it was established that Cayman weighed three-quarters of a ton.

We went into a red padded room. The walls and floor were covered with what looked like strong, thick, quilted plastic; it was surreal. Dr Gorvy said that Cayman's condition was so acute that he was immediately anaesthetised here. There was an aerial pulley system from this room to the operating theatre next door. I learned that manacles were put round Cayman's fetlocks, these were attached to chains, by which he was suspended from tracks on the ceiling and winched, upside down and asleep, into the operating theatre and gently lowered onto the operating couch.

I was surprised by the operating couch, it was also red and padded and was a deep v-shaped trough. Why had I expected a table? What use would a table be if a horse's abdomen was to be operated on? A deep v-shaped trough was such a logical design, to stop an anaesthetised horse on its back, from rolling onto its side. I felt so much better for having seen everything.

As I produced our best showjumping photograph, in which Cayman looked so beautiful, I said to Dr Gorvy:

"I bet all owners do this!" He studied the photograph and said that it was good to see a horse when it was healthy, as he usually saw sick horses. I told Dr Gorvy about our fantastic gallop in July, up the side of the cornfield on the Bradshaws when – copying "The Devils Horsemen", a team of very impressive stunt riders – I had ridden shrieking and yelping, with one hand and no rein contact at all, trusting

Cayman completely as we flew up the track, and how Cayman had slowed himself to a canter, then to a trot and a walk, before halting. Cayman was that good. I told him that I had decided to write a book about Cayman's life and promised him a copy. Finally, as we left, I gave him a kiss on the cheek "from Cayman". My friend who is a vet, once observed:

"It's not the animals; *it's the owners*!"... But Dr Gorvy's kindness did make me feel better.

Afterwards, when I went to see Sue, Cayman's vet, to thank her for making his journey to Liverpool more bearable, she told me that he would have been "as high as a kite" due to the drugs that she had given him to enable him to travel. It dawned on me that Cayman probably did not actually see very much of Liverpool Veterinary Hospital at all; so much for me seeing what Cayman saw! But going there did reassure me that he had received the kindest, most expert care possible.

Ricky had to go to Dubai. He was worried about leaving me, but booked a ticket for me to join him two weeks later. Only two weeks, but it stretched out in front of me for ever.

I went up to the stables at Gunstone to thank all of the people who had helped Cayman so much on 11th August. Will was in the tack room in Sam's part of the yard, where the competition horses and stallion live. There were tears in his eyes as we hugged each other. Sam was in the kitchen and, after another big hug, we talked for a long while. I thanked her for breaking every speed limit to Liverpool Veterinary Hospital. Sam told me that the camera in the lorry cab had enabled her and Liz, who had accompanied her, to see every time it looked as if Cayman was about to try to get down and roll in agony in the lorry and that, using the steering wheel, she had wobbled the lorry to keep Cayman on his feet. She had been equipped by Sue, the vet, with more painkiller to inject in case Cayman's pain became too severe on the journey. I was so thankful for Sam's skill, it was reassuring to know how well cared for Cayman had been on the dash to Liverpool.

Tina, the head girl, was characteristically modest when I thanked her for recognizing Cayman's colic symptoms and immediately calling the vet. I went across the lane to see Liz, and to thank her for accompanying Sam in the lorry to Liverpool. I felt like a widow visiting the principal relatives; thank goodness for relatives. By lunchtime I was emotionally exhausted.

* * * * * * *

I had an idea! I had to find one of Cayman's brothers or sisters – there must be some. If I couldn't have Cayman, then his brother or sister would be the next best thing. I knew that Cayman was bred on Anglesey; his mother's name was Dora, she was Irish Draught and his father was Thoroughbred. Cayman was only twelve, Dora may have had more foals after Cayman. I had to go to see Alison – Alison brought

Cayman from Anglesey when he was three; she sold him to me. Alison once referred to herself as Cayman's "Auntie Alison" and the title stuck. She used to live on Anglesey, Anglesey is a small place, maybe Alison would know about Cayman's family, maybe she could help me to find a brother or sister of Cayman's to buy? I went to Diamond Saddlery – Alison's business, she and her partner Mat were there. They had already heard about Cayman's death and I received more very sympathetic hugs. Alison knew that there were not many people who went out for three-and-a-half-hour hacks:

"It's such a tragedy. You spent such a lot of time together, you had so much fun; he will be *so* missed."

I explained that I wanted to trace Cayman's family to see whether I could find a brother or sister to buy. Alison looked puzzled, but determined. She got out a large blank sheet of paper and, in shiny purple ink, wrote the current year: 2006, at the top.

"Now, we've got to work back; you say it was September 1997, when you bought Cayman from me." She wrote down the year 1997, and continued methodically:

"Yes, his mother was called Dora." She wrote down the name Dora.

"I think she was three-quarters Irish Draught, one quarter Shire." I had forgotten that when I bought Cayman I *had* been told that he was part-Shire, probably because I had never had such a big horse before and preferred to forget this part of his breeding, which was a bit daunting.

"She might have been owned by John Batt, I'm not sure.

Did John sell Cayman to Ken Clwch? Ken would be about seventy now, if he's still alive. I think that Ken could have bred Cayman, but who was the stallion?" Alison racked her brains, it was so long ago and so much had happened since. The large sheet of paper was still mostly blank. Alison promised that if she remembered anything she would let me know.

I was grateful to Alison, at least there was a possibility that she might remember something about Cayman's early life on Anglesey, which would help me to find a brother or sister who may have some of his qualities.

Early each summer, Cayman's stable and turn-out rugs were sent away to be cleaned and mended. They came back in neat plastic bags with labels on: "Liz and Cayman". I put them in the garage, ready for the next winter. If it was very cold, Cayman also wore a thin fleece rug which could be washed in an ordinary washing machine. I was so glad that I had not got round to washing it in the summer – it still smelled of him. Now it was all I had left. When I felt really sad, I sneaked into the garage, where the fleece rug lay in a crumpled heap on some furniture, and buried my face in the warm comforting smell; it always made me cry, but I felt better too.

* * * * * * *

What was I doing in a tiny basement room with no windows, in a hotel in Bayswater? It was nearly the middle of September; I had to do the first part of a course to qualify as a family mediator. It was too soon, I did not want to be there, I was too sad. On the first day of the three-day course, I discovered that about half of the delegates were not lawyers like me, but psychologists, counsellors or therapists.

I have always believed that 'a problem shared, is a problem halved'; my problem was divided by twenty. There was *no one* on that course who did not know that my horse had just died. They were all very kind to me.

"Our best showjumping photograph"

Chapter Three

DUBAI

I really did not want to go to Dubai. I did not want to go anywhere, but it would be Ricky's birthday and given that he was working so pioneeringly, setting up his business there, it was only fair that I should try to be of some support to him. Despite this, and the fact that I already had a ticket, the mire of my misery was so deep that I had actually decided – on the evening before I was due to fly – that I would *not* go.

It was Judy's surprise visit, about half-an-hour after I had made my decision, and her gentle persuasion that I had nothing to lose by making the trip, which were the catalyst for it happening at all.

The day before I left, as promised, I received a lock of Cayman's mane and about two feet of his tail hair from Liverpool Veterinary Hospital. Both were carefully plaited and tied at each end with a silky, pale blue bow. They made me cry. The little piece of mane was lovely, but the huge hank of tail was macabre. It still had bits of wood shavings in it from Cayman's bed. I knew that after he had died, someone must have gathered his tail together in a bunch, held it just below the bone and hacked the whole lot off. Cayman's tail was beautiful; it glistened in the sun, the hairs at the top of each side were rippled. I wanted to see it flowing from his round, dappled rump, with the sun shining through the ends, as he walked across the field. I did not want to be holding it in my hand like this. There was something else in the big envelope. I felt inside and pulled out a tiny book of horse quotations from literature. I was amazed at the thoughtfulness of the veterinary hospital, it was just the right gift to receive now, I was grateful.

Ricky had moved to another apartment – he had been sharing before – so now there was somewhere for me to stay. It is strange to see someone you know so well, your husband in fact, transplanted to another country, an alien environment and an unfamiliar domestic setting, surrounded by recently-purchased objects which are meaningless to you. No curtains up yet and attempts at homeliness through tasteless knick-knacks given by friends who are not your friends. It is very strange; it is as if you did not know him and your past together did not really happen, as if you even imagined your marriage. My misery deepened.

Ricky tried to normalise the situation; but my

bereavement weighed so heavily, like condensing fog, that I was a dead weight. His birthday was miserable; we went out for a curry that was too hot to eat.

I woke with a start at 4:30 a.m. I thought that someone was shouting at me! It was the Mullah, in the temple opposite, calling worshippers to prayer. At 6 a.m. the automatic car wash, just outside the balcony, roared into life. After Ricky had gone to work, I forced myself to start writing my first mediation assignment. Being in a strange place with no distractions (except the Mullah and the car wash) is a great incentive not to procrastinate; there was absolutely nothing else to do.

When the mobile phone rang, which Ricky had left for me to use, it was so loud that it vibrated itself across the polished table. I had been concentrating on my assignment – it jolted me back to reality. It was Ricky, I was glad to hear his voice:

"Hi Sweetheart! How are you getting on?"

I told him that I was doing my assignment.

"Would you like to come down to The Fairmont at 5 p.m. to meet Kris and his wife Kia? You can get a taxi from outside the building, it should cost about thirty dirhams. I'll meet you in the lobby."

The Fairmont is a spectacular hotel on Sheikh Zayed Road, the main business district, and Ricky's office was there. I did not want to go. I knew that Kris was a business associate; I did not know Kris, or his wife. I did not have the psychological strength to meet anyone new, I did not have the energy to be outgoing and charming, and all the things that I would have liked to have been. I heard my voice saying: "Okay", with no enthusiasm at all.

It was 3 p.m., I did some more of my assignment, then put on my best white dress and stood on the searing pavement outside the apartment building. I was an oddity in Al Mamza Park, it seemed that there were no other Europeans there. I was very conscious of how glaringly white my limbs were in the strong sun. I stuck out one of my insipid arms, then wished I had not, as a car with writing on its side approached. It was white, and I suddenly remembered Ricky saying that only the cream taxis were licensed and insured. I need not have worried, the white car did not stop. A few cream taxis with passengers in passed by, then a free one. Good! it stopped. We drove through a really dilapidated area; I did not like the feeling of being a white woman, in a white dress, speeding in a taxi to a spectacular hotel; it felt uncomfortably colonial.

The taxi door was opened by a stately Kenyan concierge with the most beautiful shiny complexion. A group of businessmen, in long glittering white dish daks, dematerialised into one of the revolving glass doors as it sparkled round in a full revolution. The lobby of The Fairmont must be at least one acre. The ceiling was so high that it seemed not to be there. I was relieved to see Ricky waiting for me just inside the door. The lobby contained plush leather sofas and armchairs grouped around low glass coffee tables, each on a luxurious carpet – like stage sets. There must have been about eight such groups of furniture. Immaculate Philippine staff in long, crisp, white aprons, glided over the light marble floor, delicately balancing cards of matches on the edges of clear glass ashtrays, replacing minimalist arrangements of single orchids symmetrically, and aggressively plumping any cushion which might have been ever-so-slightly dented by someone's posterior.

Kris and Kia were sitting on a sofa in the middle of the lobby. Ricky introduced me to them. When Kris stood up to shake my hand I realised just how tall he was; his white-blonde hair made him seem even taller. I knew that Kris and Kia were Danish; Kris's English was excellent. They had recently married and Kia had just come to Dubai, she spoke a little English. I was enjoying meeting these new people, I was glad that I was here after all. We could have done with cool drinks, but it was Ramadan, and not quite Iftah, so we would have to wait half an hour or so until sunset to get drinks or food. We decided to stroll along the road to a neighbouring hotel, The Crowne Plaza where, Kris said, the restaurant was particularly good.

We walked slowly to The Crowne Plaza, because we were talking, but we had not walked slowly enough, because when we got there, it still was not Iftah. We sat hopefully, on voluptuous, Moorish, tapestry and brown leather sofas, right next to the café, in pole position for when it opened. We chatted, although this was not so easy for Kia, but Kris helped her by translating. It was when Kia had gone off to the bathroom, that I happened to mention to Kris that I was writing a book about my horse, who had died. Kris said that Kia also wrote books, that she was a Zen Buddhist – *and a medium ... !*

I flew into a mental panic. When Cayman was alive a very special, gifted lady called Julie Dicker had communicated with him by telepathy, at my request, to find out from him why he could not canter left, leading with the correct leg. She had asked for some of Cayman's hair to help her to communicate with him. So now, here I was with a dead horse, a medium ... *and no horse hair*! I was frantic. I told Kris of my dilemma; he seemed incredulous as he assured me: "Kia will not need any hair."

Kia returned and I told her about my book and that I had had a dream about my horse, Cayman, exactly five weeks after he had died. I described seeing him in my dream, with stretched fetlocks. I was surprised when Kia interrupted abruptly:

"Are you worried that Cayman was in pain from his fetlocks?" I was going to say that I thought that the stretched fetlocks were proof that it really *was* Cayman – because given that he weighed three-quarters of a ton, his last memory may well have been a sensation of his fetlocks being stretched, when he was suspended by them from the aerial pulley system used to lower him onto the operating couch – but I did not have chance. Kia, answering her own question, stated very definitely: "He was not."

She then said: "Cayman is here!" Kia tilted her head, concentrating hard as if receiving information.

"He has sent me a picture." I scarcely registered what she said.

Kia asked: "Have you seen a black foal running in your dreams?"

I said: "No."

"Cayman will come back to you as a black foal; you will recognize him by the white star on his forehead." I needed to record what Kia was saying; I asked whether she minded if I made notes. She said that she did not mind, so I grabbed a pad of paper from Ricky's briefcase. At my request, Kia drew the star, concentrating hard on its sides.

"You will have no doubt that it is Cayman – Cayman will guide you, you do not have to do a thing."

I felt jolted, because when I had dared to think about what my next horse might look like, I had imagined a tall, velvety black horse, leaner than Cayman, with a white star and had thought of calling him Spirit. I was crying. Kia emphasised:

"Cayman does not want you to be sad because *he will come back to you*. He loves you and he knows that you love him." My shock deepened. I was shocked that Cayman had so quickly addressed the two questions which had been hurtling around my head: Did he know how much I loved him? And did he love me? Or was it too presumptuous of a human to think that a horse might love them? I was quite sure that Cayman *had* known how much I loved him and that there was a very strong bond between us, but it was still a great relief to have this confirmed by him. Kia went on:

"It is the love between you that enables Cayman to communicate. It is *all* Cayman's energy; usually it is half the spirit's and half the medium's. He came through very quickly. He wanted to communicate with you. It *was* Cayman in your dream; that was the first time he could have communicated." Kia continued:

"He went too early, so he can come back." What I had just heard was so amazing that I felt ungrateful and pedantic asking:

"*When* will he come back?" But I needed to know:

"From about six months after the first communication in your dream, the maximum would be two years, but it will be soon."

I was extremely shocked. My sceptical, rational side was counselling me: 'Well, this is all very fine and dandy – it's just what you want to hear, but ... '. I felt as if I was being unkind and unfairly hostile to this spirit as I heard my rational side say out loud:

"Can you prove that you are Cayman?"

Now Kris was communicating with Cayman too:

"He had something like a patch or a scar on his eye." Kris pointed to the inner corner of his own left eye. *Cayman had a patch of pink skin in the inner corner of his left eye!* I felt as if the whole external world had been suspended. Ricky, Kris, Kia and I might as well have been in a bubble, sitting on an enormous, comfortable sofa on a *flying* carpet. I did not know what to do next, all I could think of was to ask another question:

"Were you born with it?" Perhaps what Kris had said had been a lucky guess! Time stopped. I did not want to hear the next sound in case it shattered everything.

"No, it started small in the corner of his eye and it was growing." Cayman's pink eye had started as a small spot on the skin in the inner corner of his eye two years earlier and had grown so that it covered about one fifth of the total area of skin around his left eye. Cayman was so beautiful; his big, calm, dark eyes ringed with black Cleopatra eyeliner, contrasting with the pure glistening white of his face. His pink patch disfigured his left eye, so I had erased it from my memory. I felt as if I had been shot in the head. Thankfully, I have never *been* shot in the head to really know what it feels like, but being reminded about Cayman's pink eye in this way caused a sudden shot of adrenalin through the top of my skull, which was excruciating. Engulfed by the enormity of what was happening, all I could do was sob convulsively. *I now knew that this was Cayman*. Ricky sat by my side in stunned silence.

My involuntary detachment was invaded. Kia laughed kindly as she reached forward and gently placed her hand on the outside of my left shin:

"Does your leg hurt? He says he hurt your leg, he's sorry. Oh! No he's not!"

The last-but-one time that I got Cayman in from the field in the evening, it was still very hot; I was wearing a dress, rather than my usual thick jeans. As we walked up the lane, we got our legs tangled up and Cayman walloped the outside of my left shin with his right front hoof. It was extremely painful; I hobbled into the yard, rubbing my leg, with Cayman walking by my side as if nothing had happened. Despite the fact that the bruise which came up was spectacular, I had also forgotten about this and was shocked to be reminded by Cayman. Kia went on:

"He says that you talked like a waterfall; sometimes he just wanted to be with nature, but he always had the sound of you talking right by him." I was embarrassed. I do talk a lot and I always talked to Cayman, both when I was riding him and when we were in the stable, it was hard not to, he was so intelligent and animated. He was easy to talk to. I asked her whether Cayman understood what I was saying:

"Of course! Didn't you see his ears twitching all the time?"

As we were on the subject of injuries, I asked:

"What was the worst injury Cayman ever inflicted on me?" Kris pointed to the outer corner of his own left shoulder.

"He says he bit you here." Where Kris was indicating on his shoulder was actually where my collar bone was fractured when Cayman and I got wedged together in the stable doorway. Kris quickly went on:

"He did something else, like little bites; he was a joker." Cayman often used to nip my bottom when I picked out his front hooves. He knew that it was unacceptable because when he was very young I had trained him not to do it. But when he was older, I knew that he did it for a joke. Also, he would sometimes nibble my back, in the way that he would mutually groom another horse.

I asked Kia which rides Cayman enjoyed.

"He says: "What I enjoyed wasn't what she enjoyed; I enjoyed just walking and talking, the two of us alone."." That was right. I certainly felt closest to Cayman when we were walking along together, by ourselves, rather than with other horses and riders. We had done lots of rides alone in the hot summer, just before Cayman died, along idyllic lanes, through corn fields and woods. As we did them, I felt those rides strengthening the bond between us. Sometimes, the bond felt so strong that as we rode along, I *did* finally stop talking to Cayman. When I did that, I felt as if we were communicating on a deeper level; it was humbling and profound … and very peaceful.

It made me laugh that Cayman had said that he enjoyed walking. I have described myself as a 'speed-freak adrenalin-junkie'. I enjoyed going fast, but I did usually feel that Cayman was cantering or galloping because it was what *I* wanted, and that he would have been just as happy to walk. He was not a horse to get excited in a big field or on a bridle path where we usually galloped. He did not buck or jog sideways in anticipation of a gallop. I prided myself on the fact that, if I asked him to, Cayman would happily walk when all around him were galloping. Now the reason was confirmed!

My next question was rhetorical:

"Did he mind me kissing him on the nose?" Kia replied:

"He wanted more!" I had not really thought that he minded. Ricky plucked up the courage to ask:

"Did he like me?" Kia replied:

"He was jealous! – he was only joking, he liked Ricky." I asked whether there were any birds that Cayman did not like; I was thinking of the peacocks on the bridle path through Long Birch, which Cayman had been wary of.

"He did not like birds that screech." It had been a screeching pheasant which had caused Cayman to try to escape into over five hundred acres of parkland as I was photographing him at Chillington. When I succeeded in stopping him – by grabbing his flapping rein as he tried to flee, so that he whirled round, his rump to me, poised for a second attempt at flight – I had been able to take what had become my favourite photograph of Cayman. It showed him looking very alert, but very confused, because I had asked him *not* to run away when he thought that there was a terrifying screeching monster in the wood to his right.

I thought that it was lovely, and in keeping with his kind nature, that Cayman then went on to tell Kia about the birds that he *did* like.

"He liked the birds to his left in the stable." She said that she had a picture of birds in clay nests, high up the wall, where it joins the ceiling. Each year swallows nest in the stables. Last summer, I had watched young swallows flying from a nest on the top of the wall, to the left of Cayman's stable.

"He says do not use a local medium." I was trying to suggest who a local medium might be, by reference to people living near the stables – not that there are very many to choose from. Harrison's person Sarah lives nearby and she is often able to tell what horses are feeling, but Kia was concentrating hard and looking quizzical, indicating that I was on the wrong track. Cayman moved on to another topic. Cayman may have meant a medium local *to him*. I had intended to instruct Julie Dicker, the lady who communicated with Cayman by telepathy when he was alive but, very sadly, she had also died in August.

"He does not mind the black cat in the stables, as long as it does not 'make a mess' in his stable. He does not like the ginger cat outside the stable yard." Kia said that she had a picture of a cat "like Garfield." Skunk is a very friendly black cat who goes into the stables and scent marks. Although I have never seen it, I am told that a large, feral, male, ginger cat visits the stable yard.

"His energy is fading, *he* wants to communicate, and it is *his* energy that is used; it takes a lot of it." Kia added:

"He says that he can communicate through Ricky; he is psychic." Poor Ricky, this came as an extra shock. Then Ricky said that he had heard his father refer to members of Ricky's late mother's family in the Caribbean having psychic powers, but that his father had dismissed them as 'mad'.

I wanted to know how Cayman could communicate with me; Kia said:

"In your sleep." I was disappointed that Cayman had not said that *I* was psychic, but after the Cayman dream that I had already had, I knew that Cayman certainly could communicate with me in my sleep.

All this shock was too much, I was crying again. Kia was so insistent when she said: "DO NOT BE SAD – YOU WILL HAVE YOUR HORSE BACK", that I wrote: "DON'T BE SAD" at the top of the page of notes which I had scribbled. I could not stop thanking Kris and Kia.

How we got to the restaurant I don't know. The lighting was low and I was sitting at a table with Ricky, and Kris and Kia, an enormous menu in my hand. It might as well have been in Japanese, I could not read it. It is not that I *cannot* read – I can! It was simply that I had developed some sort of temporary disability and my brain just could not do it. I was not functioning. Phrases were being bandied about. I heard Ricky excitedly exclaim something about duck. Kris seemed pleased by some kind of lamb. I started at the top again. The waiter returned, but was sent away as we had not all made up our minds. Eventually, everyone settled on what they wanted. Ricky moaned loudly about being "ever so hungry." I started at the top again. The waiter came back and hovered by me for ages, it did not help. By this time Ricky was "starving!" Kris and Kia had decided and placed their orders, Ricky did the same. Everyone's attention was on me. There was absolutely no point in starting at the top again. I tried halfway down but it made no difference. The waiter went away. Why do hungry men become fractious, like toddlers? It is not funny sitting next to a six-foot-two, fractious, toddler. I had a brainwave, of sorts:

"I'll have the same as Kris!"

"Hooray!" Ricky's relief was so genuine that I could nearly *feel* his hunger pangs. Fortunately, Kris had not ordered lamb, which I do not like; he had ordered some sort of fish. I ate it, but have not got a clue what it was, or what it tasted of. I was in shock.

* * * * * * *

How different I felt the next morning compared with the morning before. Cayman was coming back! I felt my psychological strength returning. Nothing could hurt me again. I was the most fortunate person in the world, my horse was coming back to me. I was so grateful. I felt calm. I rang Mrs B., my mother, and spoke to her for half an hour, forgetting that I was using the costly mobile phone. She too was amazed and thankful for Kia's prediction.

Arrangements were made for us to visit Kris and Kia at their apartment. I could not wait. This time, I would be prepared. There were so many questions that I wanted to ask Cayman. I needed to be organised, to take advantage of this opportunity. I wrote down my questions, but first – and very importantly – I wrote:

"*Thank you for communicating with me; I cannot wait to have you back, thank you for choosing to come back to me*. When you come back, I will try not to talk all the time and to let you have some peace and quiet, sorry! I could not ask very good questions last time because I was too emotional, now I have some questions."

These were my questions:

Why was it that you went too early?

When you come back will you be as tall as before?

Will your tack fit?

The veterinary hospital sent me some pieces of your mane and tail – what would you like me to do with them?

When you come back to me, what would you like your name to be?

I was going to name a star after you, should I do this or is it not appropriate now that you are coming back?

Is Julie Dicker with you? If she is, please thank her from me for her help with your cantering-left problem.

To help me with my book, what is your father's name, and what colour is he?

I would also tell Cayman that I could not wait to kiss his nose again and that I loved him.

Kris and Kia's apartment was gorgeous, so welcoming, large and bright, the walls a fascinating collage of Kia's paintings; some of people, some of buildings on the Creekside in Dubai, and lots of animals: beautiful wolves, bears and horses.

Why do women communicate so easily in kitchens? Maybe it's because kitchens are quite standard. There is usually some sort of cooker, a place for washing up, cupboards and a work surface. No matter where in the world, most women could probably make a meal in most other women's kitchens; they are a universal workshop. Of course men are not barred, it's just that they are not usually there. This might be why women often feel at ease in other women's kitchens. Anyway, my gravitational pull was towards Kia's kitchen, where she was preparing dinner. Not one to beat about the bush, and desperate to understand what had happened to Cayman, I asked:

"You know when Cayman said that he went too early, well – would he have known that he went too early?" Kia's emphatic. "Yes" surprised me, but I continued my line of enquiry:

"Would Cayman have known *why* he went too early?" I was caught completely off guard by Kia's retort, it was as if I had trespassed.

"Why do you want to know?" I was instantly confused, vulnerable and very uncomfortable, as if I had naively asked a question that I *should not* know the answer to. All I could think of to say was:

"Perhaps it was a mistake?" As if placating me with my own inadequate answer, Kia reassured me:

"Yes. Yes – it was a mistake." I had the strongest sense that the *true* reason was deep and dark and sinister and that I had gambolled innocently onto territory where I was far from safe. In a flash of silver-sharp clarity, I *knew* that it was not in my best interests to know more.

To pull myself back from the dangerous cliff on which I was teetering, I explained:

"I have had an image in my mind of a black horse running." I was disappointed when Kia declared:

"It's not Cayman; he hasn't been born yet."

But she went on:"Three horses would have you."

It was my turn to be emphatic: "*But I only want Cayman*!"

Kia reassured me that it would not be a matter of me choosing one out of the three horses, but that three horses *would choose me;* I would have all three! Before I had time to voice my concerns about the logistics of having three horses, Kia continued:

"First you will help a huge, beautiful dark brown mare called Beauty, she has had a hard life and is in Wales; she will reward you with her foal, who will be Cayman." Kia was so authoritative that I knew that what she had told me was all *already* decided and inevitable. I had a sense of something so much bigger than myself.

We had our dinner and afterwards talked around the table. I was faffing about what to do with Cayman's mane and tail. I was so frightened of doing the wrong thing; something that might stop him coming back to me. Kris's exasperation was physical as he grasped the empty water bottle, which stood on the table.

"What's the important thing? Is it the bottle or the water?" I could do this: "It's the water!"

"Right, so now all the water is gone, it doesn't matter what I do with the bottle. It's just the same, the spirit is like the water – once it's gone it doesn't matter what you do with the body."

Kris lobbed the empty bottle across the room; it landed silently on the thick carpet. I could not have wished for a clearer explanation. But I was on a roll and as if – quite unintentionally – to goad Kris, I piped up: "I was going to name a star after Cayman, but I don't know whether I should in case it stops him coming back to me." Kris's patience might have been fraying a bit.

"You can name a star after him, it doesn't matter, it won't make any difference." I decided that I definitely *wouldn't*, just to be on the safe side.

Kia told me that a young girl had been with Cayman when he had communicated with her. I was indignant – Cayman should not be with the young girl, ***he should be with me!*** We talked and talked about such wonderful spiritual things. I felt that every minute with Kris and Kia was an insightful privilege, but I did keep wondering when we were going to talk to Cayman again. I was anxious to ask all the questions on my list. The conversation took another turn, then another – and another. Finally, when I knew that it was getting very late, I plucked up courage to ask:

"Can we talk to Cayman again please?" Kia said that she needed to go and make a cup of tea. As she went to the kitchen, Kris explained:

"Kia has used all her energy." I knew that Kia would not need much energy to talk to Cayman, because Cayman would use ***his*** energy, but obviously Kia was too tired. There was nothing I could do. I was disappointed although I knew that, really, I had no right to be – Kris and Kia had already given me so much.

On the aeroplane home, I watched a film on the tiny screen

on the back of the headrest of the seat in front of me. It was "Cavalia", a moving performance by a French-Canadian troupe of people and horses. The stars being a magnificent white Andalusian stallion with a cascading mane, and a barefoot man with no shirt, who also had a cascading mane; it was set to serene music. The man next to me, who was watching an action film, must have wondered why tears were streaming down my face.

The day after I got back from Dubai, I had to go to London for the second part of my mediation training. On the train, on the way down, I read the book of horse quotations that Liverpool Veterinary Hospital had sent me. What a blessing horses are. This time I was looking forward to the course, and to sharing Kia's prediction with all of the people who had been so kind to me in my grief. I prefixed my news with:

"I'm not mad, but ..." My factual account must have been persuasive; so many people, upon hearing it, came up with their own anecdotes of 'unexplained events'. I was so relieved that sharing my good news was not difficult.

I telephoned Alison and told her excitedly about Kia's prediction. Alison was dubious:

"You do know that you're talking to the world's biggest sceptic." I could not be deflated. We made arrangements to meet for lunch. At "The Fox" there are some very big tables. The restaurant was not full and we had a huge corner table to ourselves. After we had eaten, I got out my notes and regaled Alison with my 'Dubai Experience'. As I finished Alison sat – frozen – as if turned to stone. I have never seen a person look so pale.

"... he thought that there was a terrifying screeching monster in the wood to our right"

Chapter Four

ABU DHABI

October was Ramadan, followed by Eid – in business terms a quiet month – so Ricky was home from Dubai. It was lovely being together; I hated wishing away great calendar-chunks of my life whilst he was not at home. Eid does not last forever and, at the end of it, Ricky had to go back to attend to business in Dubai once again. My ticket was booked for 21st November. In the meantime I immersed myself in the very therapeutic task of writing "CaymanStar". This time I was looking forward to going to Dubai and to seeing Kris and Kia again.

Writing the story of Cayman's life had become a really serious undertaking. I had thought that it would take me about three weeks but, as the memories of our nine years together came cascading back, I realised that my estimate was wildly unrealistic.

When 21st November at last came, it was a good job that I did have "CaymanStar" to occupy me. Ricky was at work all day in his office in the Fairmont Hotel; so I went to work with him. I had not known that it is possible to spend a working week in a hotel lobby if you don't work there, but it is.

I positioned myself in the centre of the big leather sofa in the window to the right of the revolving doors. There was not just one sofa – a matching one faced it; at either end was an armchair and, in the middle, a coffee table with an exquisite flower arrangement and compulsory ashtrays and matches, all set on an immaculate deep pile oriental rug. It was like my own sitting room, or so it seemed. The lobby is used for numerous informal business meetings throughout the day; there is a café area on the right and reception on the left. Watching the ever-shifting constellations of people of all ethnicities throughout the day was fascinating, but I wanted peace and quiet to concentrate on writing so I deliberately made myself at home, spreading out my papers over as much of the furniture as possible. As I was a woman sitting by myself, etiquette decreed that my 'sitting room' was seldom trespassed upon. Only rarely – when there was absolutely nowhere else to sit – did an uncomfortable-looking group of businessmen ask whether I minded them joining me.

A rather forward pair of South African businessmen *did* sit themselves down on the armchairs on either side of me. They could see me scribbling frantically and, jokingly, one quipped:

"Writing a book?" He seemed surprised when I said "Yes", told him its story, my reason for writing it, its title – and insisted that he promise to buy a copy. He probably wished that he had sat in the café.

There were sometimes distractions; one day I kept seeing famous people. I was trying to write and every time I looked up, there was another! It was all the more distracting because I *thought* that I recognized them, but could not quite work out who they were, so was subconsciously racking my brains trying to identify each one, when I really did want to concentrate on writing.

My difficulty arose because football is by no means my favourite thing. By the revolving glass door was a trim, bald man in a very smart suit – he looked familiar. It was not long before he was joined by a huge man, in an equally smart suit. A third man joined them, immaculate, with wire-rimmed glasses – I *did* recognize Sven Goran Eriksson. They revolved out of the door and into a big vehicle with darkened windows. As I settled down again to write, I was conscious of a stunning, tall, blonde woman with very long, tanned legs. The vertical stripes of her pink silk dress made her even more statuesque as she glided across the lobby. From the newspaper the next day, I learned that I had seen: Sir Bobby Charlton, Sven Goran Eriksson, Peter Schmeichel and model Caprice. I hoped that there would be no more distractions; I wanted to get on with writing.

Kris and Kia had moved to a villa in Abu Dhabi. All of the

villas looked biblical: white, with steps up the outside to their flat roofs, kitchens and laundries in separate buildings, all set in large, dusty yards surrounded by high white walls. One of the domestic buildings had been turned into a gallery; Kia's paintings hung impressively on its stark white walls. There was also a studio, where I walked straight to a large canvas with a pencil sketch on it, two horses: a mare and a stallion. The mare's body was turned at a protective angle to her spindly little foal. I recognized his sweet, confident expression immediately.

"You've drawn Cayman!"

"Yes" Kia said. "You remember when we communicated with him, he sent me a picture." I was curious:

"What colour are you going to paint his mother and father?" I must confess that I was testing Kia a bit; I remembered that she had already told me that Cayman's mother would be brown.

"I will ask Cayman." I was not prepared for Kia's answer. Although I suppose it made sense to ask Cayman, I do not think that this is a facility that artists usually have at their disposal. I took it for granted that Cayman would be black with a white star.

We had a really good meal; I had never eaten potatoes roasted in brown sugar before, but they were fantastic. As Kia cleared away, and Kris and Ricky stayed in the dining-room to do something on a computer, I gravitated to Kia's outside kitchen.

Kia told me that the young girl who had been with Cayman when we had first communicated with him was Cayman's sister. I was slightly confused that Cayman had a human sister. I decided that this was yet another example of boundaries in my mind being dissolved. I thought how caring it was of Cayman's sister to come with him to communicate with me. This was all new to Cayman. I did not like to think of him being frightened and was glad that his sister, who evidently loved him too, was with him.

With trepidation, I asked Kia whether we could talk to Cayman again. It's not that I was nervous of Kia – she is lovely – but whilst I desperately wanted more contact with Cayman, I was nervous of the psychological upheaval of stirring so much emotion that contact inevitably brought. I felt encouraged when Kia said that she had already "sent Cayman a message" that I would be there that evening. I thought this was very considerate of her and I hoped that Cayman did want to communicate with me again.

By now it was dark outside. Kia suggested that I go out into the large enclosed yard and call Cayman, just as I did in his field at Gunstone. It felt *very* strange to be standing under an inky-blue Arabian sky, heavy with stars, in a big dusty yard surrounded by a high white wall, calling:

"Ca-a-a-y-m-a-a-a-n! Ca-a-a-y-m-a-a-a-n!" I hoped that Ricky could not hear me, I felt a bit embarrassed. I strained my eyes into the darkness looking for Cayman's huge, familiar white shape emerging gently from the gloom, as it did when I got him in from the field in winter. I was disappointed, I could not see anything. I wanted to see him so much. I wanted to see his kind eyes gazing calmly at me, wondering what all the fuss was about. I wanted to hear the steady rhythm of his movement as he made his way to me, but there was nothing, just nebulous darkness.

"There he is! He's in the corner – there." Kia's voice was excited and positive.

"He's big!" Why did everyone always say that the first time they saw Cayman?

"Call him to you."

"Ca-a-a-y-m-a-a-a- n, Ca-a-a-y-m-a-a a-n. Come on boy, come on." I was trying, but it was hard, I really could not see anything.

"What colour is he? Is he grey like he was, or black as he will be? Kia replied:

"He is light." That did not help me to see him. By now Kia was standing by my left shoulder.

"He's here, stroke his neck."

I stretched out my right arm to where I thought Cayman's neck might be.

"I can't feel anything!"

Kia took hold of my hand and repositioned it, moving it in a long, calm, stroking movement.

"He can feel that." I stroked for a long time. I had expected to feel Cayman's hair, his warmth and the firmness of his neck muscles, but I did not. My unsupported right arm ached, I felt despondent. I asked Kia:

"Will you ask him to blow on my neck? He always did

that." Horses have an enchanting way of blowing caressing plumes of breath from their nostrils. Kia looked up, exactly where I knew Cayman's eyes would have been, if I could have seen him. She cupped her hand and very gently guided his nose (or at least where I know his nose would have been) towards my neck, whilst she coaxed him:

"Come on boy, you can do it, that's right, good boy." Kia kept on coaxing.

"I can't feel anything." I was disappointed. I so wanted to feel Cayman's warm breath on my neck again.

"He's trying – it's really hard for him." It was too much for me. As I turned away, Kia exclaimed:

"He's pawing the ground!" Now I *knew* that Cayman really was there, it was just that I could not see him. Pawing the ground is exactly what he would have done. He did not do it often but when he did do it, it was magnificent; a huge, powerful movement right from his shoulder. It was what he always did when he was frustrated and confused. I knew that he had tried his hardest to blow on my neck, and I hoped that he could feel me stroking his neck.

Chapter Five

CHRISTMAS

It was three weeks before Christmas when I arrived home from Dubai. I could not have been less interested in Christmas – I was not doing it. Christmas had become all about 'things' – gifts, objects. I had learned that things do not matter.

The comfort which Kia's prediction that: "You will have your horse back" gave me was immense, but it was still a prediction and, right now, there was a gaping, 17hh horse-shaped hole in my soul. No amount of sparkly, tinselly, Christmassy things could fill it. How could things matter when all I yearned for was Cayman?

Kia had said that it was the love between us which enabled Cayman to communicate. How relieved I felt when she assured me: "He loves you and he knows that you love him." I had learned that *all that matters is love*. I joked: "No,

I am not wearing beads and a floaty skirt." To have learned such a crystal-clear lesson was liberating; how privileged I was.

One week before Christmas, it occurred to me that if I sent Christmas cards to all of my friends who had been so kind and supportive of me, then that would be a manifestation of my love and gratitude to them. Yes, I would do that.

These would be no ordinary Christmas cards ... I needed thirty copies of the sepia photograph which I had taken at dawn of Cayman standing magnificently by the Sham Bridge at Chillington, and twenty copies of the beautiful portrait of him taken on the same occasion, when he had thought that a screeching pheasant was a monster about to come out of the woods to attack us. That picture summed-up the sweet-natured confusion which characterised Cayman's approach to life.

The photographs would not be ready until Thursday; why had I left it so late? I bought some forest green cards with an oval window that the 'bridge' photograph would slide into, and similar gold cards for the 'confusion' photograph. Our friends – such as Sam and Liz who had hurtled Cayman up to Liverpool Veterinary Hospital, and my parents Mr and Mrs B., who had dealt with everything whilst I was in Cuba: from informing the insurers of Cayman's death, to mucking-out the stable – would get the special gold cards, 'for services way above and beyond the call of duty'.

Glue, a pad of gold ink and a "Season's Greetings" stamp completed my equipment. The long kitchen table became a production line. The glue was left to set overnight and by Friday morning there were several neat heaps of finished cards.

I was very glad that I had decided to do something Christmassy. It gave me so much pleasure to hand the cards to our friends at the stables; they were pleased to have photographs of Cayman looking so beautiful. Not all of the special gold cards had the desired effect: I decided to walk two miles across the fields with Ricky, to deliver Gill's card. I was wearing my most glamorous horsey coat, with gold piping and fake fur collar and cuffs, which had never been near a horse. To avoid ripping it on the barbed wire fences I had to duck down very low. Why hadn't I given Ricky the card to carry in his large flat pockets? As Gill pulled the crumpled gold card from its crumpled gold envelope, I was sure that she could imagine how impressive it *had* looked at the start of its journey ...

From my frantically scribbled notes, made when I first met Kris and Kia, I had drafted an affidavit, which I swore before a very understanding former colleague, who is a notary public. Although I had left the firm five years earlier, I was welcomed back as if I had just returned from a two-week holiday. I was relieved. Although my former colleagues had known me to be a sane and rational person, it was with some trepidation that I had e-mailed the draft affidavit a few days earlier. It was not exactly run-of-the-mill stuff: a dead horse – Danish mediums in Dubai – the dead horse's imminent return – a black foal with a white star.

A lawyer through and through, I felt that I needed to put on record Kia's wonderful and amazing prediction, so that no one could say that I had made it all up after the event. Although Ricky, my husband, had been sitting by my side in the café at the Crowne Plaza Hotel on 24th September 2006, he was hardly an independent witness. Nothing like this had ever happened to me before; rationality had been turned on its head. My mind looped and swirled, desperately trying to make sense of it all. I had to deal with it in a way that was familiar to me. The notarised affidavit gave me a sense of security; now I could relax a bit.

I was slightly daunted when Lisa, my brother's partner, told me about Jennifer: a British Horse Society registered instructor, very proficient in natural horsemanship, a successful eventer and showjumper and groom to Olympic and Grand Prix horses, who wanted *me* to ride her horse. What a relief when I actually spoke to Jennifer on the phone. Lisa had explained my situation to her and she was so sympathetic. In her gentle southern Scottish accent, Jennifer told me that she needed someone to ride Hoss, her 17hh Cleveland Bay gelding. She also had Millie, a 17.2hh Dutch Warmblood. I would be doing her a big favour if I could go out with her on Hoss, so the two could be exercised at the same time.

I met Jennifer in the yard at her farm; she was so friendly, welcoming and pretty. Hoss was in his stable, already tacked-up, a big bright bay with a white mark on his forehead. He was not at all bothered when, still talking, we both went into the stable. Forty-five minutes later we were still talking. Hoss had got bored, stepped back so that his rump was in the corner, hung his head and dozed off.

Jennifer was so approachable and understanding, that in no time I was telling her all about my devastation at coming back from Cuba to learn of Cayman's death, my first Cayman dream, meeting Kris and Kia, and Kia's prediction about Cayman coming back to me as a foal. Telling the story drained me, but I needed to do it. What would Jennifer think? Would she still want 'a mad woman' to ride her horse? But I do believe that honesty is the best policy. I could not pretend to be anything other than in a real state: shocked and emotionally wrung-out.

As I finished my tale, Jennifer stood composed, in the deep straw of Hoss's bed, and reassured me:

"I've heard things like this before, it does not surprise me. I am a Reiki Master."

I had heard that you often meet just the right person, at the right time, when you really need them. How thankful I was to have met my good friend Jennifer.

Hoss was a bit grumpy at being woken-up, but we did eventually go for a ride around Chillington. It felt good to be sitting on a horse again.

* * * * * * *

In July, before Cayman died and before starting my

mediation training, I needed some insight into what family mediation was all about. It was suggested that I should contact Robin, the principal of a well-established local family mediation practice. I was thoroughly impressed by Robin's credentials and could not wait to sit in on some mediations at his offices.

I did not know how to dress. I thought that it would not be quite right to dress 'like a solicitor', but really my only smart clothes were sombre 'solicitor clothes'. So, I decided to put on my very smart navy blue suit and then, to look more as I imagined a mediator might look, and as it was warm, I would wear my fuchsia pink T-shirt under the jacket.

I arrived at Robin's offices a few minutes before him, they were lovely. The reception area was cosy and bright, with pleasant and smiling staff; the atmosphere was happy and calm. This was a more relaxed work environment than I had been used to. I was shown into Robin's office. Wow! Huge windows, soft yellow walls, bright modern art canvases – too many to count – theatrical brocade drapes (I was *decisively* corrected when I called them "curtains"!), inviting high-backed, deep leather chairs around a long glass table. I thought that I would enjoy working with Robin.

"*Love* the colour!" Robin, the image of an Italian profesore in his cream linen suit, blustered through the door, pointing excitedly at my fuchsia T-shirt. I was sure that I would enjoy working with Robin.

Robin took a great interest in my writing and agreed to be

a critic of "CaymanStar". At the beginning of February, knowing that Robin is from Anglesey, Cayman's home, I presented him with a quandary:

"Robin, have you got a picture of a farm on Anglesey? Or better still, a photograph of mares and foals on a farm in Anglesey? I need a photograph for Chapter One – the earliest photographs I have of Cayman were taken when he was three, and he looks too grown-up for the chapter."

Robin thought: "No, I haven't – but I know who will have!" Before he had finished the sentence, Robin's fingers were tapping away at the keyboard of his laptop.

"I went to school with Alex, I used to pull her pigtails when we were seven. Alex breeds horses on Anglesey, I'll ask her." By now both of our clients had arrived, so we got on with the mediation session.

Afterwards, Robin checked his e-mail to find a response from Alex. She had sent some photographs of her angelic little Appaloosa foals with their mothers, in an idyllic setting of lush, green, rolling pasture bounded by stone walls.

The next day was Saturday. The pictures, with Alex's e-mail address, were now on my computer. Alex bred horses on Anglesey … Anglesey is a small place ... why didn't I just *try* sending her all the information I had about Cayman's breeding to see whether Alex might know who bred Cayman? Then ... possibly … I hardly dared hope … I *might* be able to trace a full brother or sister ... another Cayman. I had nothing to lose; I e-mailed Alex.

Alex's response was prompt:

"I may be able to help you, I knew John Batt and Ken Jones (Clwch), sadly both have passed away. Ken lived at Bodernog just down the road from me. Ken was a great source of help and advice when I was starting to breed horses." It was marvellous news that Alex knew Cayman's breeder, but what came next made my heart jump ...

"I expect Cayman would have been by the dark bay Thoroughbred stallion Falconwood, out of one of Ken's Shire or Shire-cross mares."

Falconwood! *I remembered that name*! When I was negotiating to buy Cayman from Alison, she *had* told me that his sire was Falconwood and that this meant that I could register Cayman. At the time I was so bowled over by the huge, beautiful, iron-grey three-year-old, with a white tail, in front of me, that who his sire was seemed completely irrelevant. As I had never had a horse 'with papers', registration was foreign territory. But now, hearing the name Falconwood was like being thrown a lifeline – a lifeline direct to Cayman.

Alex went on: "Ken's daughter Sharon worked with him breeding the horses. I know Sharon well and I'm sure she would be able to give you more information." I was so thankful. I was halfway through e-mailing my sincerest thanks to Alex, together with an e-mail for her to forward to Sharon, when I noticed a new e-mail in my inbox. It was from Sharon! Alex had already sent my original message to her. My quest was gaining momentum. I felt myself being drawn closer to Cayman's family. I felt uneasy as I realised that throughout the nine years that I had cared for him, I had scarcely given a thought to Cayman's origins; to the fact that Cayman was part of a family, a family with a history and a future, a family which was *alive*. How important that was to me now.

Sharon's e-mail was friendly:

"Hi my name is Sharon" – and informative:

"Cayman's dam was Dora – grey mare – and the Thoroughbred stallion was called Falconwood (by Sharpo out of Treeline). Woody stands at 16.1hh ... I may have a photo lurking in a cupboard." If my heart jumped before, at seeing Falconwood's name in Alex's e-mail, as I continued to read, it stopped!

"Falconwood is still alive and well at 21 years, he is running with a field of Welsh Cob mares, Ruthin way."

Cayman's father was alive! I was stunned. Slowly it dawned on me that if Falconwood was running with mares, there might be foals ... This was more than I could have hoped for.

I had had to guess the first three years of Cayman's life when I was writing "CaymanStar", now I could ask Sharon. I asked about the Shire breeding on Cayman's mother's side of his family, about how Cayman would have been weaned, and whether he would have seen the sea from his field. Sharon told me:

"Dora (we called her 'Batt', as we had bought her from John Batt) was three-quarters Draught, one-quarter Shire. She was a star and bred us many quality stock. The showjumper, Keith Shore had a bay mare that was a full sister to your Cayman."

I was very excited about Cayman's sister. Sharon said:

"She should be called Falconwood's Briar Rose, she is younger than Cayman. Another full sister was a grey, but she unfortunately broke her leg. Dora and Woody only had bays and greys. There are many half-sisters and brothers by Falconwood. One went to Canada, as a showjumper, Foxglen Magic Feathers; she was out of a Clydesdale mare."

I felt sad that Cayman's grey full sister had broken her leg. I was sure that she would have been beautiful and would have had a lovely temperament; what a tragedy. As for Foxglen Magic Feathers ... it made me laugh to think that if I had known about the achievements of this one of his half-siblings whilst Cayman was alive, I would have expected much more from him! But I also thought what a lucky escape he had had. Cayman led a blameless life; he would not have liked to have been a showjumper, the life would have bothered him. I was glad that I had not known.

Sharon sent photographs, with a slip of paper on which she wrote: "The kindest stallion on earth – Falconwood."

The dark bay horse in the photographs was stunning. I recognized his depth of shoulder and strong hind leg. His nose made me cry; the velvety part, where the colour changed above his nostril, was Cayman's nose. Another picture showed Falconwood looking very intently at something behind him; that was Cayman's posture. It was so characteristic of Cayman that I had called a chapter in "CaymanStar", "Looking at Things". Now I knew where Cayman got this aspect of his character from.

But what about Keith Shore's bay mare? This was Cayman's full sister and I knew her name. I had to try to find her. A helpful lady in the membership department of the British Showjumping Association agreed to pass on my letter to Keith Shore. In the letter I set out all the information I had about Cayman's breeding. Although I was slightly embarrassed to do so, I could not resist sending a copy of a photograph of Cayman making a huge effort over a tiny show-jump, just in case any physical similarity reminded Keith Shore of his mare. I did also acknowledge in my letter that I was aware that he would have bought and sold a lot of horses since 1994.

I was very grateful to receive Keith Shore's answer phone message, but disappointed that – not surprisingly – he could not remember the horse.

Weatherbys were really helpful too, but I was told that:

"We have registrations of six progeny sired by Falconwood, but none born after 1994, and no mares." The National Equine Database and The Irish Draught Horse Society were equally helpful, but still no Falconwood's Briar Rose. I would have to content myself with the possibility of Falconwood and his harem of Welsh Cob mares producing a foal; at least such a foal would have half of Cayman's genes.

I had finished the first draft of "CaymanStar". All of my friends whom I had asked, had kindly agreed to be proof readers; in fact many had volunteered when I started writing. How our printer managed to produce nine copies of the manuscript, each with eighteen colour photographs, I don't know. I was thankful that it did not spontaneously combust, although there were times when it made some very worrying noises.

When I took Alison's manuscript to her, I was so happy to be able to show her the photographs of Falconwood which Sharon had sent to me. As soon as Alison saw the photographs she confirmed:

"I remember him now! – and Sharon; yes, I know her."

Looking closely at the white mark on the forehead of the beautiful, dark bay stallion in the picture, and obviously remembering Kia's prediction, Alison exclaimed decisively:

"*There's your star*!" I corrected her:

"No, the star is going to be on the foal's forehead."

* * * * * * *

At the beginning of February, Kris told me on the phone that Kia's painting of Cayman was now on her website. I remembered the pencil sketch and could not wait to see how it would look painted. I had a surprise. Cayman, as a foal, was painted bright bay; he did appear to have a white mark on his forehead. He was very sweet and definitely Cayman, but I was confused by his colour. I sent an e-mail to Kia:

"When we first met and Cayman gave you the picture, I remember that you said that he would return as a black foal with a white star – that's what I wrote down; but in the painting he is bay! Why isn't he black? Please let me know."

I was anxious. I did not want to upset Kia, I had been so comforted by the information from Cayman which she had passed on to me and so grateful to her, but I really needed an explanation. As an insurance I did, however, emphasise:

"I will, of course, love him whatever colour he is!" I did not receive a reply.

* * * * * * *

After Kris had succeeded in finally persuading me that it really did not matter what I did with Cayman's tail, I decided on a very appropriate use for it. Spring came early, it was warm and bright and Ricky was home from Dubai. I often walked down bridle paths which Cayman and I had ridden; this made me feel closer to Cayman and peaceful. Ricky did not like me going walking alone. He had a point; whereas I felt very safe on the back of a 17hh horse – which anyone with bad intentions would probably be frightened of anyway – on the ground, on a remote bridle path and with no martial arts skills, I was vulnerable. But the energy of this morning, with its brilliant blue sky and chirping birds, compelled me to sneak quickly out into the garage whilst Ricky was concentrating on his work, stuff my feet into my walking boots, jump into the car and be halfway to 'The Long Mile', Cayman's and my favourite place, before Ricky would notice that I had gone.

I had Cayman's tail with me, all apart from a slender lock which I had re-plaited and re-tied with the pale blue ribbon. I now knew, from Kia, that Cayman liked birds. It was quite clear from their frenzied chatter that the birds were avidly nesting. What better building material than Cayman's tail? I knew that it was the right thing to do with it. From the bridge, with its ornamental balustrades, where Cayman always liked to graze, I meandered down the paths through the trees to the right of the true bridle path.

When I had met Kia for the second time, at her villa in Abu Dhabi, she told me that if I asked Cayman to walk with me in familiar places, he would. As I walked through the wood, in my mind I asked Cayman to guide me as to where to walk, strewing his tail as I went. I would not have been at all surprised to hear the sharp metal-on-stone sound of him tripping on the path because he could not be bothered to pick his feet up properly as he walked. I knew that I was not at all alone as, like an equestrian Ophelia in reverse, I strewed the tail hair, a few strands at a time, into the air to be caught on branches and in bushes.

We, or rather I, reached the lodge at the Coven-end of 'The Long Mile', but there was still a lot of tail left. I walked back up to the bridge, this time along the paths through the trees on the opposite side of the bridle path. By the time I reached the bridge, I still had some tail. I decided to go up 'Corris's Galloping Field' where, on Christmas Day two years earlier, Corris and Cayman surprised Mrs B. and me with one of our best-ever gallops; the result of synchronised, uncorrected disobedience, which neither Mrs B. nor I would have wanted to correct; a gallop which neither of us would ever forget. By the time I reached the top of the field all of the tail was gone.

A few days later, when Mr and Mrs B. had walked down 'The Long Mile', they told me that there was no Cayman tail to be seen. Good! Now it was all usefully enmeshed in birds' nests in our favourite place – I felt settled.

Chapter Six

THE BLUE CROSS

I am sure that when my friend Susan was in practice as a criminal lawyer, her male clients must have thought that they were being *rewarded* for their misdemeanours. In fact, they were probably planning their next 'taking and driving away' to ensure further meetings with their advocate. You see, Susan *is* glamour: iconic bone structure, rock-chick blonde hair, alabaster complexion, couture scarlet lips, cut-glass accent with husky, bluesy undertones. I know no one else like her.

Just before Cayman had gone on loan for a year to Rodbaston Agricultural College, when he was ten, Susan and I had taken Corris and Cayman out for a ride; it was a beautiful summer evening. A former eventer and show-jumper, Susan had not sat on a horse for years, so for safety she rode Corris who, at 15hh, was much smaller than Cayman. In no time Susan was cantering Corris round the indoor school as if she was in the collecting ring at a competition. You really don't ever forget how to ride a horse.

When we arrived at The Blue Cross Equine Welfare Centre, by appointment, on a day when it is not usually open to the public, Susan – in her shades and dramatic black poncho – could easily have been mistaken for an animal-loving multi-millionairess benefactor, probably from New York.

When Susan had suggested the visit, I had debated whether to go at all. Equine Welfare Centre? It sounded grim. I visualised horrific sights of poor broken-down sad horses: ribs sticking out, sunken backs, hollow eyes, matted coats; innocent victims of human abuse, neglect and cruelty. I was not sure whether I could cope with seeing that; I knew that it would affect me deeply and I was still so wounded by Cayman's death. But something was gnawing away at my mind; what if there was a foal? Maybe a poor starved mare and her little foal. It was early May after all, some foals had already been born. What if there was a mare with a little black foal, with a white star? I had to go.

As the centre manager showed us into an immaculate, vast and airy new crew barn with spacious loose boxes down either side of a wide gangway, my trepidation vaporised. This was fantastic! There were not many horses inside. In his enormous box, with its soft, clean wood-shavings bed, a cream-coloured pony who was recovering from laminitis looked like royalty. My anticipation rose as, out of the corner of my eye, I caught sight of a very big, bay horse in the loose box in the top right corner. I was not listening to what our guide was telling us. Was that horse a mare? Was there a little black foal, on wobbly legs, just out of sight, somewhere behind her?

"Oh that's Hamish." Our guide had followed my gaze. "He's been in for the farrier."

"Do you ever have any foals? Or mares and foals?" I needed to know, I could not stand the suspense.

"No – not usually; we get more adult horses." I was relieved. Now that I need not be constantly on the lookout, I could relax a little. The loose boxes all had doors in their back walls. When we went outside we saw that these led out into small woodchip paddocks where horses who could not go out to graze could exercise and get more fresh air. There were two outdoor manèges and a large, bright, indoor school – all as immaculate as the crew barn.

Still no gruesome sights. With their perfect post and rails fencing, the picture book paddocks, each with a field shelter, contained groups of three or four horses. What lovely horses! This was nothing like I had imagined. Whatever had happened to them previously, they now wanted for nothing and it showed in the aura of contentment that blanketed them as they purposefully mowed the pasture together as a team, stood snoozing nose-to-tail, or mutually groomed – relieving each other's itchy withers with an intensity that no amount of brushing by a person could ever achieve. These horses were peaceful and happy.

We thanked the centre manager for such an enlightening visit. We wanted to make a big donation, we both knew how much it must cost to keep so many horses this well. We gave what we could afford; perhaps our host was surprised that Susan did not donate an art collection, or an oil well ...

I could not stop thinking. I had been told that The Blue Cross did not usually have foals. That did not mean that they never had foals. What if they did get a foal? I sent an e-mail; again saying thank you for our visit, complimenting the staff on the condition of their horses and the immaculate stables and paddocks, and requesting:

"I should be grateful if you would kindly add my contact details to your database, just in case a 16. 2hh+ mare with a foal, or a weaned foal to make 16. 2hh+, needs a home."

Soon afterwards, I was very efficiently sent re-homing forms. Ah! a problem – the forms again asked about the type of horse to whom the applicant wished to offer a home: age, size, capability, etc. But what would I do if, having completed the form, stating that I wanted a foal to make16.2hh+, I received a phone call: "We've got a foal, *she's chestnut* with white socks."? I could hardly say:

"No. My foal is black, with a white star ...!" A phrase about gift horses and their mouths sprang to mind. But equally, I could not complete the forms with specifics, that would sound ridiculous too. I was, unusually, stumped. I decided to keep the forms, in case I could pass them on to someone else, and to continue to hope that I could rely on Cayman's assurance that I did 'not have to do a thing' and that he would 'lead' me to him.

Chapter Seven

FALCONWOOD

"Don't go to see him until he's lost his winter coat", was what Sharon had told me in February. "He's not so young and he doesn't keep his winter rugs on, he'll look rough now." I could not wait to see Falconwood – 'Woody' as Sharon called him – but I made myself wait until he would have lost his winter coat. I knew that even Thoroughbreds can look like shaggy bears in winter, if they live out. Anyway, I thought, if I am going looking for a foal, there will be no point in going too early in the year.

Sharon gave me the telephone number of Falconwood's keeper, Mr Jones. In late May I rang to ask whether I could visit Woody. As there was no one in, I left a message. After a few days and, as I had not heard from Mr Jones, I rang again. The phone was answered. Mr Jones was "up the field, or in the shed." I was talking to his son.

No matter, I could ask him whether there were any foals; he would know.

"I don't have anything to do with the horses, I'm more interested in machines," was the reply. Thwarted. The suspense was intolerable. Mr Jones did return my call; I was out:

"Yes, you can come and visit Falconwood", my answer phone said. Phew! I was relieved, but I did not have the address. After I had left some more answer phone messages (by now I had come to the conclusion that Mr Jones *lived* 'up the field' or 'in the shed'), Mr Jones rang me one morning. I could not have wished to speak to a more peaceful, patient man. By now I actually already had his address from Sharon and had mapped out the directions to his farm. When I informed Mr Jones that one of the road numbers which he gave me was incorrect and substituted my own suggestion, even though it was the road on which the farm where he had lived for his entire life was situated, he was forbearing, suggesting:

"Well, perhaps if you remembered the two numbers ..." Now was my chance to ask whether there were any Falconwood foals. Mr Jones' kindly response was not 'no' and it was not 'yes'. I was too emotional to ask about foals by any other stallion that Mr Jones might have. I was no further forward, but I *was* going to see Cayman's father. Finally, I would have the honour of meeting Falconwood. In itself this seemed like a miracle, I yearned to set eyes on him. Sharon counselled me: "Don't expect him to look a million dollars; but you will see what a gentleman he is."

Saturday 2nd June 2007 was bright and sunny. My father Mr B. had agreed to drive to north Wales. After all that they had been through in handling the practicalities of Cayman's death whilst I was away in Cuba the previous August, it was very important to me that my parents came to see Falconwood. I asked my brother's partner Lisa to come too. It was with Lisa and her mare Hattie that Cayman and I had gone 'on holiday' – well, for two nights – to Felindre in mid-Wales; we had enjoyed that so much. Lisa is a qualified riding instructor and very skilled in natural horsemanship. I thought that her presence would add a bit of 'normality' to this grieving family. But as we got closer to Mr Jones' farm, just to make sure, I reminded everyone:

"Even if, when we get there, we see a black foal with a white star, *do not react*. Just act normally, no spooky business!" I was afraid that if Mr Jones learned of my quest for the predicted black foal with a white star – *and had him* – then either he would be unwilling to sell any foal of his to a lunatic, or the price may go so sky-high that, having found him, I could not afford to buy the foal. I tortured myself with worry and hoped that my stern briefing would safeguard my bargaining position, as simply a bereft owner making a 200-mile round-trip to see Cayman's father – which, to a north Wales horse breeder, was probably lunacy enough anyway.

I was so distracted that it was not until we had spent an hour getting lost down some beautiful steep lanes that I remembered that I had got directions from the Internet with me. We found Mr Jones' farm on exactly the road he had said it was on. Mrs Jones was in the porch, she called out into the yard: "Terry – your visitors are here!" and indicated:

"He's in the shed." As I walked towards the shed, a polar bear came round the back of the enormous horse wagon which was parked in the yard. Terry was tall and robust, with thick white curly hair and white stubble. He had a calm and accepting air about him. We were welcomed and shown into the kitchen for tea; there was plenty of room for us all around the big table.

I had brought photographs of Cayman: our best show-jumping one, taken when he was eleven, showing the kindness and concentration in his big, liquid-dark eyes and his huge, shiny, white knees as he sailed over the fence; also the photograph of him on the beach at Ynyslas, with his horse friends: Harrison, Toby and Lucy, in characteristic 'looking at things' stance; as I now knew, just like his father Falconwood. Terry studied the photographs:

"He's a nice horse!" An opinion worth having.

The first field that we went into was at the back of the farm, a big steeply-banked pasture of mares, yearlings and one very young foal – not black. There were two big horses, about 17hh, one chestnut, one black.

"Those are half-brother and half-sister to your Cayman," Terry explained. I was amazed. These were the first relatives of Cayman's whom I had ever seen. I hugged the huge, black half-shire gelding – he had Cayman's peacefulness. I could tell that he was used to being hugged.

In response to Mr and Mrs B.'s and Lisa's questions, it was interesting to hear from Terry about his horses, but I asked few questions and did not take any photographs. Where was Falconwood? I was on tenterhooks. Was I just about to see the little black foal with a white star? Was Kia's prediction about to come cascading to fruition, engulfing me? Would I have Cayman back in the next moment? It was hard to 'act normally'.

Terry led us down the steep narrow lane. I had worked-out that, as with anyone who has something impressive to show, he was saving the best until last. It was a lovely afternoon; we turned down another lane – where there were still late bluebells in the hedge-bottom and the hawthorn was in blossom – and stopped at a five-barred gate into an idyllic, banked meadow of lush grass, liberally sprinkled with buttercups and daisies. We could see the first field in the distance and Terry's white farmhouse, with its grey roof. There were no horses in the field. Terry whistled.

It was like a film … a *magnificent* dark horse, lithe and fit, with a fast, active pace, trotted up the steep bank from the bottom of the field. He had a striking, broad white star on his forehead, *which I recognized* – I was spellbound. His herd fanned out behind him: half a dozen elegant, fine-legged Welsh Cob mares – one with a tiny spindly little foal, another with a slightly older foal. I could hardly believe that *this was Falconwood*! I was in awe. He was beautiful.

Falconwood came up to Terry at the gate and allowed him

to rub his face and neck. There was a calm relaxation about him; although clearly in charge of his herd, Falconwood moved amongst the mares and foals with kindness. The herd stayed at the top of the field as we all leaned over the gate and Terry told us about the mares and foals; one was only three weeks old, the other three months. I needed to get closer to Falconwood, to actually touch him would bring me closer to Cayman; I needed to do that.

Having no experience of stallions, I was unsure how Falconwood would react to an intruder in his field. Terry assured me:

"He's kind in the field, provided no one tries to take any of his mares away." I was happy to climb over the gate, but Terry opened it for me. I walked quietly into the field and meandered my way towards Falconwood, hoping that he would understand from my unthreatening approach that I had no evil intentions towards any of his herd. I stretched out my hand as I gently approached. Falconwood was unconcerned and continued grazing methodically, whilst also keeping a watchful eye on the mares and foals. When I felt the warmth of Falconwood's muscular neck under my hand, my heart leapt. Finally – finally, I was touching the life that gave Cayman life, his foundation; how crucial that was for me.

I needed a permanent record of this beautiful horse, so I set about taking photographs but, by this time, I had attracted the attention of the elder of the two foals, for whom I was very obviously a novelty. He would *not* leave me alone. He kept getting in the way, popping-up between me and

Falconwood. He had no fear whatsoever and was *insistent* that I should pay him attention. Like a 'power ball', the more he was rebuffed, the more energy he bounced back with. I had never come across an animal like him before. Finally, I shooed him away back to his mother and resumed my photography. I concentrated on Falconwood and the clever things that my digital camera could do – I was happy that I was getting some good pictures of this magnificent horse. But then, as I was bending down, my thoughts projecting through the camera lens to Falconwood's noble head, I was brought swiftly back to earth by gentle, repeated tugging of the bottom of my hair, which is long and was loose down my back. It felt as if someone was trying to attract my attention, but why would they be doing it like that? Then the thought that someone was playing a practical joke flashed through my mind. As I stood up and turned round, ready to remonstrate with my assailant, that it is not easy to take good photographs when your hair is being tugged, I was surprised that there was no-one there … except the insistent foal.

Lisa explained that what was really funny for everyone else, watching from their vantage point by the gate, was that the foal had crept up behind me – from right across the field – with his mouth open all the way, until he got to my hair. It must have reminded him of a horse's tail.

I thought that this was so funny and so sweet that, as he had now got my attention, I stroked him. He was covered in bright orange wool – there is no other description for his coat. His legs were black and white, in alternating horizontal stripes, his orange-tipped mane stood up vertically and fluffy orange tassels protruded from his ears. He was ridiculous – but he did not *know* that he was ridiculous. His silly, innocent confidence was compelling. As I stroked him he nipped me: my bare arms, my stomach, anywhere. I retreated to the gate to talk to Terry, but 'monster foal' was not going to be deflected. He followed me to the gate, turned round and squashed his orange back end into my hip; I *had to* scratch his rump. I did feel sorry for his mother. She was standing quietly, watching from the edge of the field; a pretty, bright-bay mare. Her long-suffering, patient expression, seemed to say:

"I do hope that my baby is not bothering you too much; but it is *so* nice to have a rest." With trepidation, I dared myself to ask Terry what her name was. His response was not "Beauty", but I was too anxious to comprehend what it was. Strangely, the second I did not hear "Beauty", it was as if my mind shut down, although I do remember Terry telling me that she was six.

As soon as I had seen the foal, I had decided that he was not Cayman. He was not black with a white star, but I needed to make absolutely sure, so – knowing that he would probably follow – I walked away, out of earshot of Terry, and said to the foal:

"Look, if you are Cayman you've got about thirty seconds to prove it! If you are, scratch behind your ear with your back hoof. I know that you're only little and it will be hard, but just *try*." Cayman could do this. The foal didn't; he just carried on trying to nip me, which hurt. To discourage him, I flailed my arms like a windmill. Initially, he looked surprised, but in no time he had worked out the pattern of my flailing and still managed to nip me by darting his nose out, in between flailings. His persistence indicated that he seemed to think that this was quite amusing. Eventually, he did tire of the game and went off, back to his mother; however she turned her hip to him and raised a hind leg, warning that she was not yet ready to be bothered by him again. I watched as a couple of his 'aunties' gave him the same rebuff and then, completely undaunted that everyone had sent him away, he backed-up to the trunk of an old tree and stood wiggling his orange rump exaggeratedly against the abrasive bark, with the most nonchalant self-possessed expression, as if to say:

"So! – you think you don't want me do you? You'll see ...!"

I went back to Falconwood, he looked so wise and kind. I kissed him on his neck and told him that I had had one of his sons – Cayman – who was marvellous. I thanked him for Cayman.

We had been looking at his herd for about an hour. Now Falconwood had decided that it was time to move off down the bank, towards the open gate in the bottom corner of the field, which led to the field from which they had come. Terry said that there was a stream at the bottom of that field; what an idyllic environment this was. The herd moved slowly and purposefully to the bottom corner and through the gate. Falconwood stood by the gate waiting until the last mare, who was slower than the rest, had gone through, then he lifted his head to look at us for a moment – before turning his back and walking through the gateway, out of view and into the next field.

What an exit! I was in awe of Falconwood's magnificence. I had to remind myself that, whilst it was Falconwood whom I had come to see, he was ***not*** the horse I was looking for.

In the car on the way home, I asked Lisa:

"What did Terry say the mare was called?"

"Bonnie", was Lisa's reply. The insistent foal did not have a name, so I made up the name 'Woody Baby'. He had made such an impression on me – I could not forget him.

I was confused; the elements of Kia's prediction seemed to be all mixed and muddled up. As we drove home, I tried to make sense of it all. Falconwood was ***nearly*** black and he certainly had a very noticeable white star, but he was not a foal. The foal, whom I could not forget, was not black – but he ***did*** look like the foal in Kia's painting. Kia had said that when I saw Cayman, I would have "no doubt". Now I had lots of doubts, so I decided that the foal could not be Cayman. Again, I was emotionally exhausted.

The next day I telephoned Sharon to tell her that Falconwood had not looked 'a million dollars' – he had looked '***two*** million dollars'.

My best friend Judy is very wise. I told her about

Falconwood and Woody Baby – and my confusion. Judy already knew about Kia's prediction:

"Do not be restricted by it. Spiritual things are sometimes not meant to be taken so literally," she said. "That little foal was trying to tell you something." But what if I bought him and then the real foal appeared? Or, what if I bought him, stopped looking – and missed the real foal?

Kia had said that I did 'not have to do anything', that Cayman would lead me to him. I was sure that Cayman *had* led me to Woody Baby, so why was he not black? The sequence: Robin, Robin's friend Alex, Alex's friend Sharon who is Falconwood's owner, Falconwood to Woody Baby – it could *not* be a coincidence. So how could Woody Baby not be the right foal? It could not all be a waste of time and effort.

I was covered in bruises again. In the long, mirrored wardrobe doors in the bedroom, I could see bruises from horse-bites all over my body: two on the back of my right arm, one in the middle of my chest, another on my left hip. It reminded me of the previous year, just before I had gone to Cuba, when I had had to account to a vigilant practice nurse for five bruises – all caused by Cayman. I was back to normal!

"This was Falconwood!"

"He kept getting in the way, popping-up between me and Falconwood"

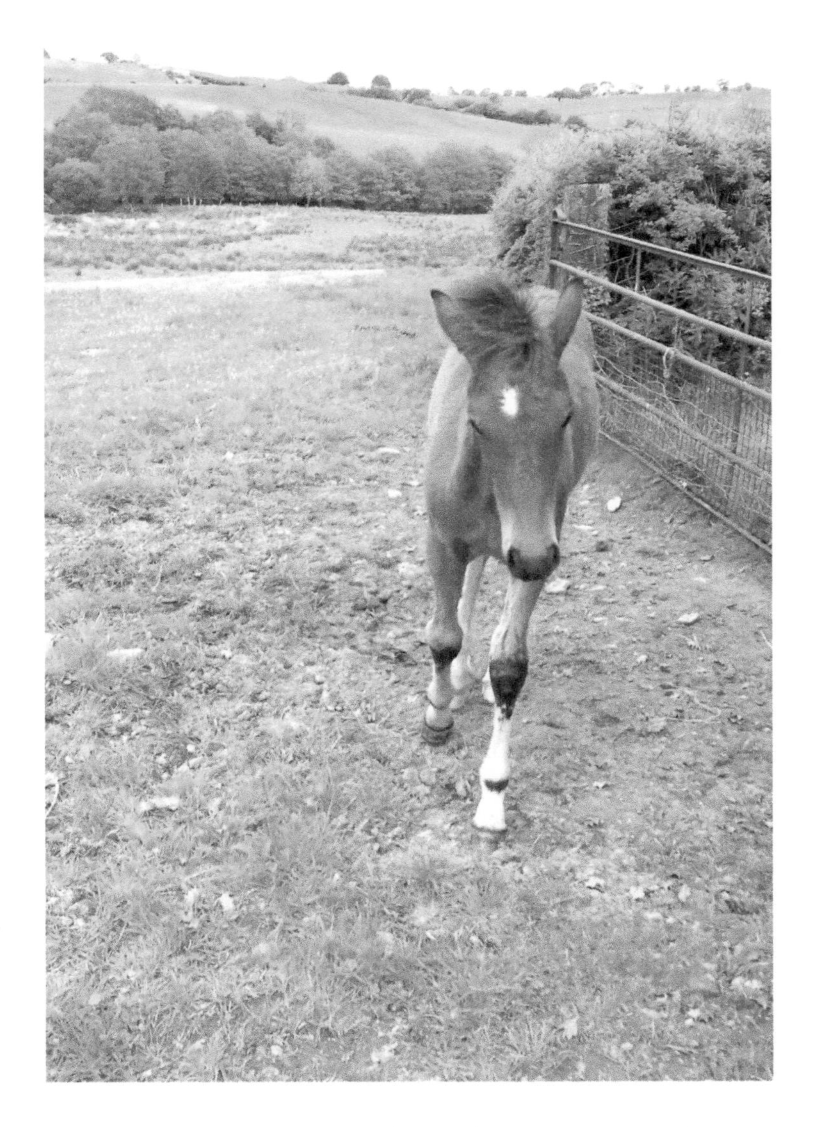

"He was *insistent* that I should pay him attention"

Chapter Eight

BEESTON CASTLE HORSE SALE

"Liz, I've *got to* go to Beeston Castle on Wednesday!" Not all of my friends are called Alison, in fact only two of them are; it was Alison W. who rang me on a Tuesday in mid-June. She said that twenty years ago, when she had re-found her horse at Beeston Castle after six months of looking for him, she had had exactly the same feeling. This time I was the one looking for a horse, but I decided that even if it was Alison having this feeling, it should not be ignored. I felt that I should go, so Alison and I made arrangements to go together; I was excited.

That evening, something dawned on me: what if I found the foal, or the foal and his mother? I had to make contingency plans, and quickly, in case I needed to bring them back with me from the sale. I rang Sam at Gunstone and told her my dilemma:

"I have hardly got enough room for my own mares and foals! – I suppose he could go out with our foals." Okay, I had the 'weaned foal contingency' taken care of, but what about the other contingency? Jennifer's husband is a farmer. Although farmers cannot see the point of horses – no milk, no fleece, we don't eat them – she said that he agreed to let me bring a mare and foal to the farm as a stop-gap, until I could fix up permanent livery elsewhere.

I had to be prepared. Transport from the sale should not be a problem, there would be lorries either going home empty or delivering horses which, for the right price, could make a slight detour. When Alison collected me, she was not surprised by my bucket containing: head collar, lead rope, tail bandage, travel boots – and carrots. Equipped with riding hat, gloves and body protector, I had even remembered my cheque-book.

Never having been to Beeston Castle before, the unfamiliar routes added to my excited trepidation. The car park was nearly full, a vast potholed expanse of concrete, Tarmac, grass and gravel. All types of equestrian and human transport, from luxury to barely roadworthy. With the atmosphere of a fairground, a bustling market selling brass ornaments, giant car-washing sponges, bacon, perfumes – in fact absolutely everything – formed an incongruous buffer between the car park and the long, low, unhappy sale buildings. I did not think that this was a place which any horse would like to be in. A horse who found himself here was probably unwanted; not a good position for a horse. As I entered the sale buildings, my trepidation grew; a chill had come over my excitement. The dismal grey of the concrete floor, the endless, ordered, metal railings forming row upon row of small pens; every surface hard, restraining, alien, awful. What a grim place for a horse.

It was a small sale; only a fraction of the pens were occupied. I walked quickly up and down the rows of pens – hardly daring to look. All I was doing was searching for a little black foal with a white star, hoping that I did *not* find him here. When my patrol proved to me that, indeed, he was not here, I could breathe again. But, as I went round the pens for a second time – more slowly – I knew that I must not allow myself either to touch any horse, or to look into his eyes; and certainly not to do both. Jennifer's husband might not have been happy to accommodate a herd of horses.

"Liz! Come and have a look at this one!" Alison called me over to a pen at the end of the row nearest to the entrance to the sale ring. In the pen was a very dark bay, light-boned gelding with a fine, pretty little head. He wore a bridle and had a severe bit in his mouth, the reins were looped around the back of the over-long saddle which he carried. Because he could not extend his neck, the poor horse was forced to stand with his nose tucked-in and his neck arched. Anyone who did not realise what stress – and therefore pain – this artificial outline put on his neck and back muscles might have been impressed by his appearance, but his eyes manifested his unhappiness. In an attempt to avoid his restraint he incessantly bobbed his head, making it difficult to gauge his age by looking at his teeth. However, as a former R.S.P.C.A. inspector, Alison was deft. The incisors were short and straight.

"No more than three," was our consensus. Like a spider monitoring unwary insects attracted to its web, the seller appeared with a passport for a five-year-old horse (usually worth more than the same horse at three). The passport showed a photograph which, at first glance, might have been of the horse in front of us. When we queried the age, we were assured:

"Yes, he is three, the passport office made a mistake; you know how easy it is to get numbers wrong!"

Alison and I decided to sit by the sale ring. I was confused by the prices; what looked like a nice 17hh Cleveland Bay hunter made £720, the same as an in-foal jenny donkey. I was glad that I was not buying. Alison and I admitted to each other that we were both waiting for the dark bay gelding to come into the ring. We waited ... 'very safe coloured Cobs' … 'eventers' … 'hunters' … 'sports horses' … more 'coloured Cobs' … No fine, dark bay gelding.

As we left the sale ring, via the route by which we had come in, we hardly recognized the horse in the nearest pen. His tack was off and he was calmly pulling at a heap of haylage. He had a bucket of water, and a girl with long red hair was quietly talking to him. His eyes were settled – he was content.

The girl told us that the week before, her mother's horse's laminitis had become so chronic, that he had had to be put down. They desperately wanted to give a home to a dark Anglo Arab – and now here he was! He did look as if he *knew* that he had been fortunate that day; and … the name which they had *already* chosen for their new horse was the name which was on the passport that accompanied him!

We looked around the market stalls. Now that I felt more relaxed I could appreciate the wonderful, fragrant, ripe strawberries being offered at a price which seemed to be in a time warp. I even felt frivolous enough to look at a shoe stall. For two years I had searched for some stylish trainers. Now, in my size, I found a pair of bright turquoise patent and suede designer trainers with Velcro straps. Yes, from that description they might sound weird but they were exactly what I wanted – and were practically being given away. I was happy to be bringing home two blue shoes and not two horses.

By evening I was tired. I questioned myself: why was I glad that I had *not* found my little black foal with a white star at the sale? Why was I relieved? I knew the answer. It was that, really, I did not want *any* foal, I wanted a foal by Falconwood. That was very important.

Chapter Nine

HALLELUJAH!

The day after the horse sale, I was brushing my hair in the mirror – and monitoring the development of my 'Woody Baby bruises' – whilst in my head reciting in German: 'Mirror, mirror on the wall', from Snow White:

Spieglein, Spieglein an der Wand,
wer ist die Schönste im ganzen Land?

It always made me laugh, because the German word for fried egg is very similar to the word for mirror. I was daydreaming when, from nowhere, an *imperative* command came into my head.

"Go and look at Kia's painting."

Urgently I flicked all four switches, turning on the computer which lurked, oafishly, under the desk in the study. Why was it always such an effort for it to stagger out of its slumber? Why was its brain so slow? I thought that it was supposed to be razor-sharp technology. I did not have a lot of time for it, but conceded that it did sometimes have its uses. It whirred grudgingly. I logged on as fast as I could. Five green lights shining on the router, I was in business. Kia's website sparkled efficiently into life. Into "Gallery", into "Animals", down, across, there it was … "Hey Cayman". Electricity in *my* brain sizzled for a split-second as the pathway of realisation seared its course, then … BANG! a firecracker of revelation. It *was* the foal; *it was Woody Baby!* All at once I was overwhelmed with happiness, relief, invigoration, excitement, love. Destiny had clicked into place. I had the final piece of the jigsaw. All of the elements of Kia's prediction had been in front of me, it was just that I had not recognized them. Woody Baby *was* Cayman. *I had my horse back!*

Ever analytical, and to try to organise my reeling mind, I made a list of 'Objective Evidence': Falconwood was a dark horse with the white star on his forehead, which Kia had drawn for me. The bright bay Cob-type mare and her bright bay foal in Kia's painting were just as in real life. When I had first seen the painting, I had dismissed what I thought was the romanticised setting of a foal, mare and stallion, all in the same field, but at Terry's farm that was how it was. Woody Baby was with his mother in the herd headed by his father, Falconwood. Even their field was the same as in Kia's painting, strewn with bands of yellow flowers and, in the distance, a white house with a grey roof – Terry's farm house, there it was in the painting too! Kia said that the mare would be in Wales … definitely. And her name … doesn't 'Bonnie' mean 'Beauty' anyway? Kia had told me that Cayman would lead me to him. In September 2006 when I had asked Alison – who had originally brought Cayman from Anglesey – about his breeding, she had forgotten almost everything. But then, in February the next year, when I had asked Robin whether he had a photograph for Chapter One of my book about Cayman's life, the sequence of introductions was like dominos pushing each other over; it had its own momentum – and it had led to Woody Baby.

I wondered whether Woody Baby's coat would turn dark. His orange fur certainly had very dark roots and foals do change colour – often several times – before their final colour emerges. Woody Baby could become very dark, and he too had a white mark on his forehead.

Next, 'Subjective Evidence': Woody Baby's *insistence* was compelling. He confidently attached himself to me (literally, when he wanted his rump scratched), simple as that. There was a quirkiness about him; his innocent self-assurance and the cheeky way he had nipped me whenever I had tried to send him away. He was a joker … I felt that we *already* knew each other.

I could not dial Terry's number fast enough – not in! I left a message: "I would like first refusal on Bonnie's foal." That should clinch it. It was Thursday, but by Friday I was surprised not to have heard from Terry. I'm no good at 'playing it cool', or strategies, or any of the things which make a good poker player.

"I would like to *buy* Bonnie's foal" was Friday's message; I also asked whether it would be convenient for me to visit again on Sunday. No reply from Terry elicited two further, increasingly frantic, messages on Saturday. Anxiety was well and truly in control, batting my thoughts about like a malevolent feline with its paw on a terrified mouse's tail. What if someone else had already bought the foal? It was probably a good job that Ricky was in Dubai, I was so anxious that I was not fit to be with.

I rang Terry just after 7.30 a.m. on Monday: "You should have just come on Sunday," was his good-natured, accommodating response. Terry was obviously proud of Bonnie's foal:

"I think he's going to turn into a very nice horse."

But in response to my request to *buy* his foal, I was totally floored when Terry said: "I had not thought of selling him." This was not a possibility that I had even considered; my proposal was totally confounded. But this was the only horse on earth that I wanted; he had gone to so much effort to come back to me – it could not all fall at the last hurdle. Whilst my brain whirred I chattered inanely to Terry. I don't know what I said but benevolently he suggested:

"You can come and see the foal again." Phew! A chink of light, a way forward, a possibility … a hope.

"… look at Kia's painting"

Chapter Ten

REUNITED

Wednesday 20th June was the day when I would go back to north Wales to see Woody Baby. How could I wait? To make it more real I drew round the date on the calendar, now the date stood out. I had made it *look* like a special day – I hoped that it really would become one.

I always approached Wednesdays with trepidation; ever since, aged eleven, I had had a four-hour cookery lesson on Wednesday mornings. Cookery was not a problem, I liked cooking. It was not even the cookery room, a far-flung outpost past the swimming pool and dining hall (chlorine and cabbage). No, it was the teacher. Terror incarnate: prim and crisp with her bright auburn 1940s hair and sinister vermilion lipstick – she looked cruel. My instinct crystallised when she reduced a sensitive boy in the class to tears. In

1971 boys *really* did not cry. Thereafter, that was Wednesdays dismissed as ever being good days.

On Tuesday afternoon, this Wednesday started to shape-up true to form:

"I've got a meeting tomorrow in Nottingham." Ricky announced. As he was away in the Middle East so much, he had decided that rather than watch his car decompose at home, he would sell it. So, we shared one car. One car which *was* going to north Wales on Wednesday. The meeting was important – I would have to make other arrangements. I would have walked to north Wales.

Alison W. wanted to see Woody Baby; she had a vehicle. I would ask her whether she would like a 200-mile, six-hour round trip to stand in a (possibly wet) field for an hour and be bitten by an orange fluff-ball with an exaggerated idea of his own importance. Alison was keen, but not sure whether she could take a day off at such short notice.

I needed a contingency plan. Perhaps I could use my mother, Mrs B.'s car. I rang – my father was in:

"Yes", but it would involve him taking her to where she had to be on Wednesday.

"Why don't I take you? It would be simpler." My very kind father *did* know what he was letting himself in for, having already been to see Falconwood.

At 8 a.m. on Wednesday Alison rang to say that she could not go to north Wales. By 9.30 a.m. I was on my way – with Mr

B. I felt sick and hollow inside, like before an exam for which you know you have not revised enough. I was setting off on a quest: to buy the only horse on earth whom I wanted – who was not for sale – and I had to come back home with a promise from his owner that when he was old enough to be weaned, he would be mine. If this was a fairytale, at least I would have been given a magic cloak or something. No matter – I had a magic prediction. I kept focused.

We could do with some lunch. Llangollen had become the centre of the universe; no point in even trying to park, let alone get into a café. We carried on to Corwen which was quieter. I have noticed that somehow men have a knack of choosing meals from menus, which are very good value. Mr B.'s roast pork dinner was worthy of a banquet, and freshly cooked … that was the problem; so freshly cooked that it took nearly an hour to arrive. My tuna sandwich was not fast by any means but was finished without a trace, probably before Mr B.'s dinner was anywhere near the cooker. The knot in my stomach was tortuous. Eventually we left Corwen – only another fifty miles to go before my fate was sealed.

Terry, as affable as ever, welcomed us in for a cup of tea. We talked: 'around the houses' … 'up the hills' … and 'down the valleys' even … for ages. Evidently, it was for me to commence negotiations. How hard it was; I attempted to put on my 'lawyer hat':

"Just pretend you're negotiating a financial settlement in

a divorce," I told myself – "You've done that plenty of times." No, that didn't work; somehow it just was not the same. Here I was, sitting with a very sympathetic and kind horse breeder, in a welcoming farm kitchen, on top of one of many endless, lush, grassy hills … it was not the same at all.

Eventually, and with an attempted veneer of nonchalance which I'm sure fooled no one, I forced myself to say something banal like:

"Well, what about this foal then?" There! I had done it! There was no way back. The roulette wheel in my mind spun into life with the velocity of a hurricane: red-black-red-black-red-black. A blur … fate ruled.

The smile spreading across Terry's face was compassionate and there was a kindly, toying expression in his eyes as he drew deeply on a roll-up and then exhaled:

"Well, I had my plan, see. I had my three-year-olds, I had my two-year-olds, I had my yearlings and I had my foals; then someone came along and messed it all up."

Jackpot! Woody Baby *was* for sale! After not very much negotiation, Terry suggested the exact figure that I had decided would be a fair price. What a relief – I very nearly bit his hand off. No strategy, no:

"Okay – but you deliver." Just:

"DONE!"

I floated down the lane to the field; I *do* know what walking on air feels like. As soon as Woody Baby saw us, he walked purposefully up the bank, towards the gate and straight to me. He must have felt the intensity of my relief torrenting over his furry little body as I hugged him.

"Pick his feet up." I thought that Terry was joking:

"You pick his feet up," I joked back. Why would I risk picking up the feet of an unhandled, four-month-old flight animal in the middle of a field?

"No, really – he'll let you." Terry was convincing. I positioned myself quietly by Woody Baby's nearside shoulder and gently ran my left hand down his front leg, whilst reassuring him:

"Good boy, easy lad, come on – up!" Sure enough, his knee bent and a tiny hoof slid into my hand. Carefully, I lowered it back on to the grass. At the back, the same again; and on the other side. What trust, what confidence, what calmness the little foal had about him. When Mr B. guided Woody Baby's muzzle onto his own shoulder, just by his neck, Woody Baby was happy to stay there – contentedly dozing.

When it was time to go, Woody Baby pressed his chest to the five-barred gate as we looked back into the field from the lane. His fine, alert head was high, his eyes engaging and his mobile ears pointed to where he wanted to go – and with whom. But he was a bit ahead of himself; it was another six weeks or so before he could be weaned, so he would have to stay where he was for now – it was paradise after all.

The journey home was lovely; a golden glow cast by the mellow, low sun made this an enchanted Midsummer's Eve.

The next day I attended a course at Shugborough Hall, a

beautiful, white, Georgian mansion, just outside Stafford. Being in that setting, amongst such interesting people, was privilege enough, but when it came to introducing ourselves to each other, the inspired way in which we were asked to do this was to say something really good that had happened to us in the past week. How wonderful it was to be able to say:

"Yesterday I bought a foal. He is the half-brother of my horse Cayman who died tragically last August. He is the only colt foal by Falconwood to have been born this year. I have called him Falconwood CaymanHavana. *He really is the only horse in the world for me.*"

The End

"He must have felt the intensity of my relief"

Chapter Eleven

EPILOGUE

I visited Woody Baby often until he was weaned. I was with him on my birthday in July, Cayman and I had gone for a magical ride, drenched in sunshine, on my birthday the previous year. But most importantly, we were together on the date in August when Cayman died, only one year before. How could there be any pain? There was only happiness – my horse had come back, and so soon … just as he said he would.

Now, I would not change a thing. I am humbled that Cayman has taught me the most crystal-clear lesson I have ever learnt. That lesson is about love – and its *immense* power.

Falconwood CaymanHavana on 11 August 2007

Chapter Twelve

CAYMAN DREAMS

On 15th September 2006, my life took a new turn. Exactly five weeks after he died, I had my first Cayman dream. It was quite different from any other dream I have ever had, in fact 'visitation' would be a better description – the communication was so strong, so clear and so memorable.

I had a distinct feeling that this was the beginning of something, I was *sure* that Cayman would communicate with me again. He did! In fact I was amazed at the frequency of his communications, not only with me but also with three other people close to me. Everyone has emphasised the extraordinary clarity and strength of their Cayman dreams, and how well they remembered them.

Cayman also let me know that he was there, in some other surprising ways ...

In the following pages, the communications are described.

What is most wonderful is how truly reassuring those communications were for me, which I am certain was their purpose. Quite simply, Cayman's kind nature continued to manifest itself.

LIZ'S FIRST DREAM

Cayman appeared from round a corner by a low, old redbrick shed, in a paddock. He seemed very relieved to see me again. He approached me and communicated plaintively that he had been "taken away" and that "experiments" had been done on his fetlocks. The bone below each fetlock joint (the last joint in a horse's leg, above its hoof) looked disproportionately elongated, as if it had been stretched; he had great difficulty walking because of this.

Cayman was slightly dazed, as if he had just woken up. I was aware that he had been through some sort of process, from which he had just emerged, and that this was his first opportunity to communicate.

Elizabeth Brown
15th September 2006

RICKY'S FIRST DREAM

Whilst Liz was in Dubai with me, I had a dream that I was in the porch of Sam and Will's house, at the stableyard at Gunstone, and that I was handing over £130 to Sam, for her to collect another horse.

Liz's riding things were also being transported. They were in a heap on the yard and included tack and a lungeing whip; my walking boots were there too.

Although I did not see Cayman, he communicated very clearly to me that we would "ride again very soon".

Richard
29 th September 2006

LIZ'S SECOND DREAM

At home, I had gone to bed feeling sad generally about lots of things, including the tragedy of Cayman's death. In my sleep Cayman comforted me; I did not see him, but I had no doubt that it was him. He made me feel cared for. I woke up feeling much better, and stronger.

Elizabeth Brown
10th October 2006

LIZ'S THIRD DREAM

I was about to be kissed by my favourite, very attractive – if rather flamboyant – male comedian. His lips were enormous – the size of a cinema screen. Because of their size, he had great difficulty controlling them; the concentration required to shrink them and target them onto my own lips made them quiver absurdly. As the lips homed in, I realised that they were not human lips … they were pale grey, with pink patches, velvety and whiskery … they were Cayman's lips. In a very camp, theatrical way he said:

"If you're going to be like that – I don't think I'll bother coming back!"

I woke up worried, until I realised that this was Cayman's idea of a joke. I had been getting too serious and sad, thinking about him too much the previous day. When he had communicated with Kia, Cayman had emphasised that I should not be sad and Kris had told me that Cayman was "a joker". It was appropriate that he appeared as my favourite male comedian.

Elizabeth Brown
17 th October 2006

LIZ'S FOURTH DREAM

I had this dream immediately after a bad dream.

Cayman was tethered by his reins to a metal barrier on the pavement outside a local school, by a busy road. Crowds of children were leaving the school and thronging the pavement; there was a lot of traffic – it was mayhem.

Cayman was standing patiently waiting for me; he was calm. As I approached him, I remembered that I had left him there the previous night. I felt guilty that I had forgotten him.

Cayman was glad to see me and we walked off down the road together. I wondered whether Cayman was thirsty and hungry – I thought he must be. Cayman was happy to be walking by my side. I was leading him, rather than riding him, and was happy to have him by my side – although I did feel guilty about leaving him tied-up overnight. As we walked, I felt that Cayman was escorting and protecting me.

Elizabeth Brown
17th December 2006

JUDY'S DREAM

Although I have been a close friend of Liz's throughout the time that she owned Cayman, I had never had a dream about him before.

I was with Liz, Ricky and Liz's parents in a house with a field at the back of it; everyone was in the kitchen preparing food. Liz asked me to get Cayman in for her as she was busy. I'm not at all used to horses and was very apprehensive; I could see Cayman in the distance, at the top of the field.

Cayman knew that I was unsure, and told me not to bother about getting him in, but to look after the foal; he did this humorously – implying that I would not be much good at getting him in anyway!

Not in the field, but close to me – near the back door – there was a newborn foal without its mother. I moved the foal to a trough of warm water – which was in the rear part of the kitchen, but out of Liz's sight – and carefully sponged it down; I thought that this would be like its mother licking it.

The priority, according to Cayman, was to care for the foal.

Judith
23rd December 2006

UNEXPLAINED EVENTS (1)

Judy visited us this evening. Ricky and I had both been through our garage during the day, as we had been out walking and it is where we keep our walking boots. The front and back garage doors are kept closed and no one else has access to the garage. The bucket containing Cayman's grooming kit is also kept there. Shortly after Judy arrived, I went into the garage to get some potatoes. I was shocked to see that the sponge from Cayman's grooming kit was very noticeably in the middle of the garage floor. Judy confirmed that in her dream (23rd December), she had used a sponge to bathe the foal.

Elizabeth Brown
30th December 2006

UNEXPLAINED EVENTS (2)

i) Yesterday I rearranged Cayman's bridle and two head collars securely under his saddle (which is stored on the saddle-rack, on the garage wall). The weight of the saddle sitting on top of them kept them in place. When I went into the garage this evening, I was shocked to see the two head collars in the middle of the floor.

ii) This morning I dusted the pictures on the wall going up the stairs, and made sure that they were all straight. This evening, I came upstairs to the study. About an hour later, immediately I went on to the landing to go downstairs, I was taken aback to see that the large picture of Cayman was crooked by about 30°. The other eight pictures (which are not of Cayman) were all straight. Ricky had not come upstairs in the meantime and neither of us has ever knocked a picture on the way up the stairs, as the handrail keeps us away from the wall.

Elizabeth Brown
15th February 2007

EDWARD'S DREAM

I found myself in some familiar stables. I don't know where the stables were, they only felt familiar. I was wearing my riding gear. I continued in with a sense of purpose but not knowing what that purpose was.

I walked down the row of stables until I came across a horse who had got out of his stable. I went over to put him back in; I approached him cautiously. As I got closer, I could see that he was a small, thin horse with a blanket on. I recognized him to be a young Cayman (well as young as I've seen him in photographs). Before I got to the horse, another horse who was black with a white star on his forehead and fully tacked-up, came charging down the row of stables and hit me very hard at full speed and with all his weight. I then felt his lips on my shoulder and neck, very briefly because the shock of the impact had woken me up.

When I had fully woken up, I could still feel the horse's lips on my shoulder and neck; it was a feeling that lasted for a very long time. I felt that the second horse had also been Cayman and that I needed to go and tell Liz as soon as possible.

Edward
2nd April 2007

RICKY'S SECOND DREAM

Liz and I bought a house, a light and airy barn conversion a short distance from a village, and were showing Liz's 'horsey friends' around it. I then realised that I was no longer in the house but that I was inside Cayman as he took Liz for a hack in the countryside. After that, we were both riding Cayman; I was sitting on his back, behind Liz. I was tiny. I felt as if my body was combined with Liz's, and as if both of our bodies were combined with Cayman's. Cayman was huge and had wings, we were moving extremely fast, just above the ground. I asked Liz how I was going to get back to the new house, 75 km away. I then found myself at our present home sitting on the sofa talking to our friend.

I had this dream in Dubai at a time when I was very stressed, having narrowly escaped a serious road accident that day. I felt that Cayman empathised with the problems I was facing and that he was saying that it was time for me to go home to Liz. It was a reassuring and comforting dream.

Richard
6th April 2007

LIZ'S FIFTH DREAM

Cayman was in a pen made from bales in the middle of a very large, high barn. He had come back to me. He was fully grown and grey. I was worrying and fussing about whether he was hungry and had enough to eat. He could communicate with me in English and I could reply in English; he understood exactly what I was saying. Cayman assured me that he was fine and that I should stop fussing. I hugged Cayman and he hugged me by putting his neck and head around my back.

Cayman came into and went out of the pen at will. Some of the bales had been pushed off the walls, it was very 'tumbled-down', but he always returned to it voluntarily. This proved to me that he was back permanently.

Cayman's big black saddle had been put away uncovered, it was thick with dust. I said to Ricky that the saddle-rack on the garage wall, where it was stored, was too high up, and that saddles should always be put away where you could reach them. I got out my smaller, old brown saddle and put it on another rack, below the big saddle, as I felt that I would soon be needing that one too.

This was a very reassuring dream which made me feel very comforted by Cayman, happy and peaceful. It was less clear than previous dreams and more remote, but the feeling of comfort was very strong.

When I woke up, I could feel an aura of reassurance, comfort and love around me. Its depth was about an arm'slength all round. It felt dense. *I have never felt more loved.*

Elizabeth Brown
17th May 2007

LIZ'S SIXTH DREAM

Cayman and I were at home; it was somewhere high and fairly treeless with rolling hills, like upland mid-Wales. It was late-afternoon and warm; I had finished physical work for the day. Cayman was dappled grey, sleek and fit, with his summer coat – a bit fat – as when he was twelve.

Wearing T-shirt, jeans and trainers I jumped onto him bareback. Even in my dream I knew that I should have on my hat and boots.

We played on a steep field; we were both having fun, trotting and cantering. I was thinking: "What if I slip off him?" – his back and shoulders were so sleek – but I did not. We moved in complete unison, as one, very tightly and safely together. We were both enjoying ourselves; riding bareback was easy.

When we halted, Cayman arched his neck and brought his head in. From his back, I leaned forward and was hugging his head and neck. I heard him say:

"I love you." I was surprised, thinking: "Horses don't talk!" Then, as if to address my surprise, Cayman said again, but far more clearly, so that I had no doubt: "I love you."

Up the mountain road in the distance, I saw a young woman whom I know, walking to church in the next valley. I was surprised that she had the energy to do this, because she had been frail and ill. It was as if her energy came from the church itself, and the warm welcome that she knew she would receive there.

As I woke up, I felt loved and reassured.

Whilst I was having this dream, I was aware that it was a dream; its quality was different from previous 'Cayman dreams'. It was less direct, but the "I love you" communication from Cayman – particularly the second one – was very clear and very direct.

Elizabeth Brown
7th July 2007

CAYMAN'S EYE

In the nine years that I cared for Cayman, I saw him from every angle. When you groom a horse and handle him for years, you know what every part of him looks like. That's why, at the beginning of July 2006, I was shocked when – as usual – I stood behind Cayman in the stable about to groom the top of his tail, and looked forward along his right side, to his head. Cayman's head was slightly turned towards me, so that he could look behind to see what I was doing.

The reason I was shocked was because when I saw the side of Cayman's face, I did not recognize him.

His eye was different. It wasn't the right shape. Cayman's liquid-dark eye was so open that it was almost square – calm and trusting. The lid of this eye was heavier, so that the outer corner curved seductively as it tapered. It was sensual, darkly mysterious and alluring.

I was disturbed – it was not Cayman's eye. Confused, I moved urgently to the front of him, where I was reassured to see Cayman's soft, familiar eyes again.

I pushed the uneasy feeling caused by this experience to the back of my mind; I didn't know what to do with it. It stayed there for a long time – no less uneasy – until, in July 2008, realisation hit me … I had been shown Falconwood's eye.

Elizabeth Brown
August 2008

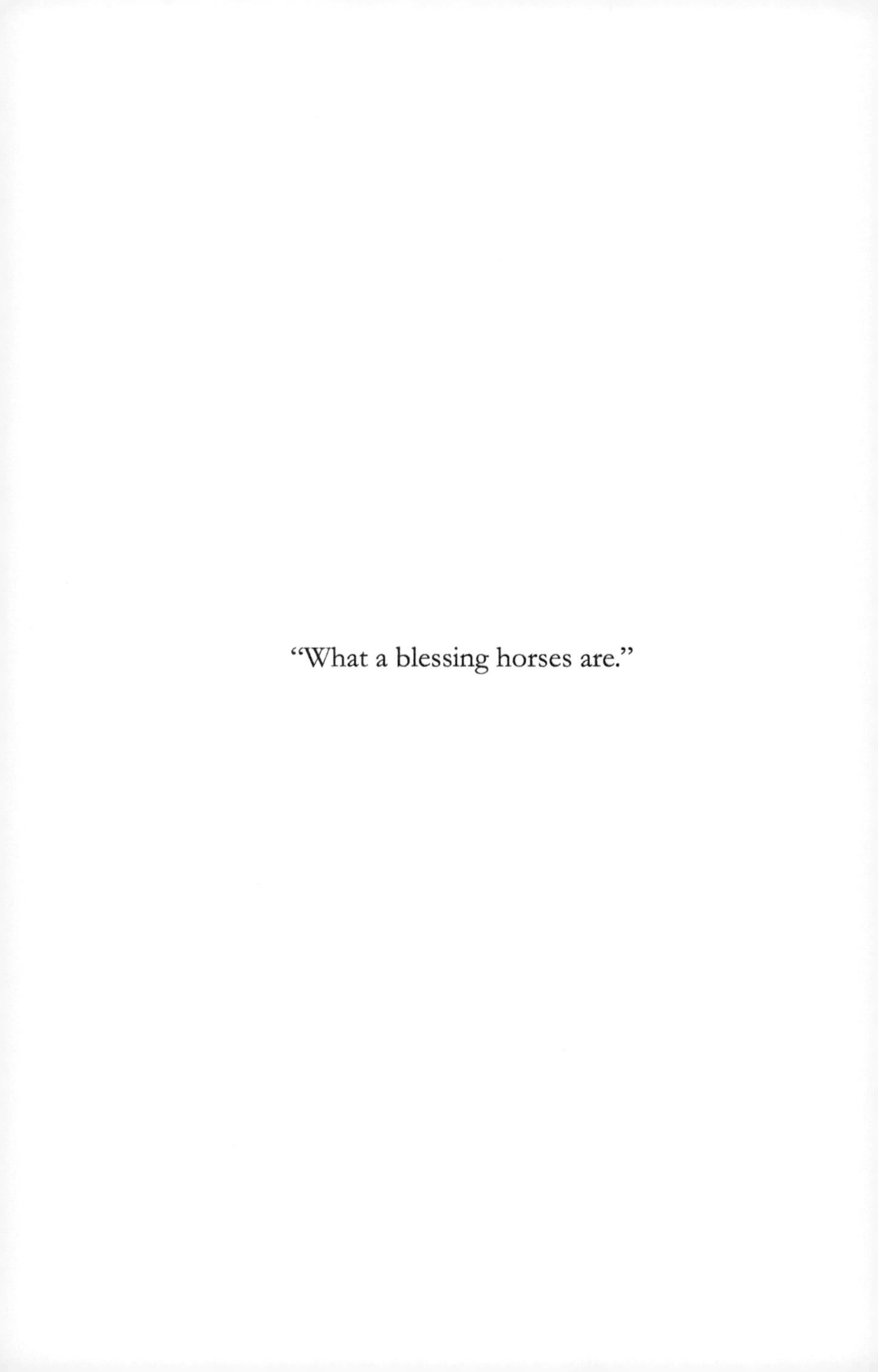

"What a blessing horses are."

If you enjoyed *CaymanHavana*,
read Elizabeth Brown's first book,

CaymanStar
The True Story of a Horse's Life

When Liz walked up the footpath from the bridge over the stream, to find her way blocked by the most enormous and most beautiful horse she had ever seen – who happened to be standing there, dozing magnificently in a sun ray – she had no idea what an incredible, life-changing journey was just beginning.

Told through a horse's eyes, this true story – often humorous, sometimes sad, always empathetic – chronicles the growth of a deep horse-human bond over nine years, from an unpromising start, to a profound union. A bond galvanized on very long rides in all seasons and all weathers: exploring and getting lost, holidays by the sea and up mountains, gallops in sunshine which were better than flying.

"In *CaymanStar* the character of Cayman comes out very strongly to make it a thought provoking and actually humbling story. It did help me a lot; as a new horse owner I found comfort in knowing that Cayman's owner had faced problems – and solved them. It's also very funny in places, I laughed out loud quite a few times!"
Susan Chambers M.A., FCIPD